The White Horse

ALSO BY DIANE THIEL

Echolocations

Writing Your Rhythm:
Using Nature, Culture, Form and Myth

Cleft in the Wall
(chapbook)

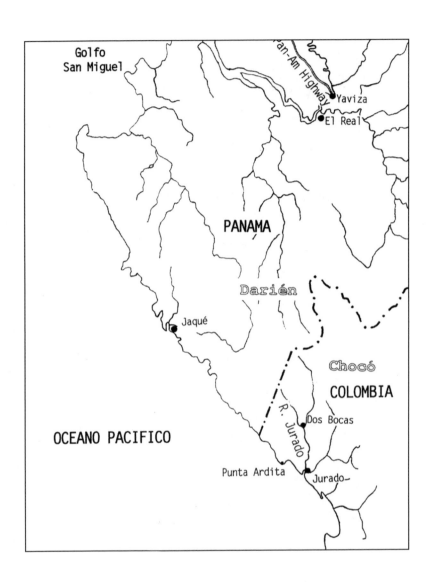

The White Horse

A Colombian Journey

DIANE THIEL

etruscan press

All photographs by the author.

Etruscan Press
P.O. Box 9685
Silver Spring, MD 20916-9685

www.etruscanpress.org

1 2 3 4 5 6 7 8 9 0

Publisher's Cataloging-in-Publication
(Provided by Quality Books, Inc.)

Thiel, Diane, 1967–
    The white horse : a Colombian journey / Diane Thiel.
    p.cm.
    ISBN 0-9718-228-9-1 (pb)
    ISBN 0-9745-995-2-2 (hc)

    1. Thiel, Diane, 1967——Travel—Colombia—Pacific
Coast Region. 2. Rain forest ecology—Colombia—Pacific
Coast Region. 3. Pacific Coast Region (Colombia)—
Description and travel. I. Title.

F2281.P23T45 2004   918.61'504635
                         QBI03-700586

Designed by Elizabeth Woll

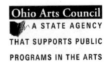

Ohio Arts Council
A STATE AGENCY
THAT SUPPORTS PUBLIC
PROGRAMS IN THE ARTS

*The Ohio Arts Council helped fund Etruscan Press with state tax dollars to
encourage economic growth, educational excellence and cultural enrichment
for all Ohioans.*

The slight boat slides through earth and time…
The voice travels on, leaving the mouth behind.

(from Eduardo Galeano's
"Story of the Wandering Girl Who Traveled
into the River and up the Night")

ACKNOWLEDGMENTS

Excerpts from *The White Horse* have appeared in *The Miami Herald, The Notre Dame Review, Brown Alumni Magazine, The Connecticut Review, Artful Dodge, Mi Poesias,* and *Louisiana Literature.* My thanks to the editors of these publications.

I am grateful to Anthony Walton, who first helped me envision the shape of this book and then read several drafts and offered keen editorial advice. My gratitude also to Phil Brady, Kathryn Kruger, and Dana Gioia. Thanks also to Ana Maria Tierra and to all the people mentioned in these pages who opened their homes and their hearts to a traveler.

And finally, thanks to my family and especially to my husband, Costa, who in so many ways helped me stay on the road to completing *The White Horse.*

for CH, whose initials
appeared in my cup

and for my son,
whose initials will be known
at the time this book appears

CONTENTS

ONE

The Bridge

A strange sound interrupted my tossing. I went to the window, the cold air against my eyes. At first I saw only starlight. Then they were there. Up in the March blackness, two entwined skeins of snow and blue geese honking north, an undulating W-shaped configuration across the deep sky, white bellies glowing eerily with the reflected light from town, necks stretched northward. Then another flock pulled by who knows what out of the south to breed and remake itself. A new season. Answer: begin by following spring as they did—darkly, with neck stuck out.

— WILLIAM LEAST HEAT MOON,
Blue Highways

1

I saw the first white horse on the road from Costa Rica to Panama. We were taking the twenty-hour bus trip through the mountains, and it was close to midnight. Like most of the passengers I had fallen asleep, when something woke me suddenly. I looked out the window. Running beside the bus was a white horse, keeping pace with us, its long mane flying out behind. I turned to wake Ana Maria, wondering if I was dreaming, but she was already staring out the window herself. When I looked back, the horse had disappeared.

It was almost Christmas. We would be going through Panama and traveling on to Chocó, the Pacific Coast rain forest of Colombia, to visit the Emberá tribe. Most of the tribe lived in villages on the frontier of Panama and Colombia, and we were headed for those located particularly along the Jurado River. We had brought with us several bags of books: twenty copies of *Donde no hay Doctor* (Where There Is No Doctor), a water pump, and three microscopes, which Modesta, Ana Maria's Emberá friend, had requested for the detection of malaria in her village.

Ana Maria, with a Colombian mother and an American stepfather, had grown up in both places. For the past few years, she had been traveling back and forth from the States to small villages in the jungle, organizing grassroots groups for environmental work in Colombia. She had asked me to go with her this time to see for myself the conditions, to see the DDT still being used, to see the rain forest being cut down faster every day, to see the villages caught between two worlds, villages where there is no running water or refrigeration but a generator powers the new television of the richest man in town.

Ana Maria and I said nothing about the horse for a few minutes. Then she told me what the children say when they hear thunder: "There goes Santiago's horse."

"Who's Santiago?" I asked.

"He is more than one man, more than one story," she said. She paused for a moment and then added, "You might meet him in Chocó."

Through the window of the bus, I could see the constellation of Pegasus in the sky, the mount of poets, originally the carrier of thunder and lightning for Zeus. I fell back to sleep thinking of Santiago's horse and of the legend of the horse-fountain, Hippocrene, which bubbled forth from the mark made when Pegasus' hoof struck the earth.

2

I AWOKE AGAIN an hour or so later, this time not to a horse but merely to the jolt of a huge pothole that knocked my stomach into my throat. Ana Maria slept on undisturbed, her head leaning slightly on my shoulder. Inside, the bus was still, and I could almost feel the wheels moving counterclockwise underneath. I looked out the window into the dark forms of the trees, half-expecting another vision.

We were probably close to the border with Panama. The whole journey had seemed driven by chance, even my decision to go. I had felt compelled to join Ana Maria on this trip. A few others had planned to come as well, but as it was to be during the Christmas holiday, they had backed out as the plans became firm. But I had nothing to hold me. Family might miss me, but I had spent other holidays away, partly, I admit, to avoid the stress of family gatherings and expectations. I had also recently lost a serious relationship and wanted to put it behind me. The Christmas season in our culture is not one to weather alone, and particularly not for the freshly wounded. But as William Least Heat Moon put it, someone "who couldn't make things go right could at least go."

The moment Ana Maria had asked me, I knew I was going. She always had such an intensity when she spoke about Colombia. I heard the urgency in her voice when she spoke about the changing conditions there, the thousand-year-old trees being taken for lumber, the indigenous people's cultures being destroyed along with their homes. It made my problems feel small by comparison.

Although I had traveled in South America and would go on to spend many months of future years in Costa Rica, Nicaragua, Bolivia, Peru, Panama, and Colombia, including several trips to the Pacific Coast rain forest (the particular region we were heading for), this journey would be different. It would be the one that would open the way for me, that would give rise to so many questions and have a profound effect on my ethics. It was the first white horse, but it wouldn't be the last.

And Ana Maria would be part of the magic. She simply drew adventure to her. From the moment I met her, Ana Maria struck me as far older than her thirty years, eccentric yet childlike in her exuberance. I admit that some people with her eccentricity had struck me as too "New Age," too insubstantial, too eager to latch onto something, to borrow others' religions. But Ana Maria was unlike anyone I had ever met. Her spontaneity and elfin spirit captivated me.

On the night we met, I had gone as my slightly skeptical self to a full moon celebration on Miami Beach because I'd been asked to read some of my poetry and I liked the venue. Ana Maria was on the program, playing panpipes. When I met her before the show and was introduced as a poet, she asked to hear a poem. I recited her a short one that I had been working on just that week.

"Oh, I know that one!" she said.

I was ready to correct her. How could she? But she continued, "I will play your poem as the song it was a thousand years ago." And she winked at me, lifting the pipes to her lips.

3

WE CROSSED THE border to Panama at one in the morning and obtained a visa from the tiny office there, which the official opened just for us after some serious begging. We had to hurry in order to catch another bus to Panama City, where we were to take a small plane to Jaqué in the Darién region—wild coastal jungle. The tiny bus was filled with locals—we had not taken a tourist route. Ana Maria and I were doubled up in seats, with our luggage hanging off the roof and the microscopes held gingerly between our legs.

We weren't really sure what to do when we reached Panama City. We didn't know the plane schedule or where the airport was. I sat next to—almost on top of—a thin young Panamanian man by the name of René, who began asking me questions in Spanish. I was worried at first, with all of the money I was carrying in my belt: at least a thousand dollars. Ana Maria and I were bringing money to encourage the Emberá people to make crafts for sale as an alternative to cutting down the trees. We both had much more cash on us than our shabby exteriors suggested.

"Where are you bringing those?" René asked, noticing the microscopes poking out of our bags.

"Darién," I answered.

"Darién?" he seemed very surprised. "What are you doing there?"

"An environmental project," was all I said, tired from traveling. I wasn't really in the mood for conversation, at least not about what Ana and I were doing. "What do you do?" I asked.

"I'm studying *biología*," I thought I heard him say.

"Oh, so you must know quite a bit about Darién," I commented, "about the plant and animal life there."

He paused a moment, as if unsure how to answer. "Yes," he said, "but I've never been there. Are you two going alone?" René seemed to disbelieve that two women, not to mention Americans, would be traveling off to the jungle alone, and he appointed himself our guardian, at least for the day in Panama City. It wasn't until a few hours later that I found out that he had said he was studying *theología*. It was an interesting misunderstanding considering that he had agreed that his field gave him an extensive knowledge of flora and fauna.

When we arrived in Panama City, René invited us home to his mother's place, which was very close to the bus station. They lived in the tiniest of units—one room that had a toilet and shower behind a curtain and a kitchen area with a stove but no refrigeration. Several pictures of Christ and the Holy Family were covering the places where the peeling paint was the worst. A few neighbors had seen us and wandered out of their apartments to see what was happening. René's mother welcomed us with smiles and acted as if she knew we were coming.

"How was your trip?" she asked. "You must be tired. Rest. Rest." She offered us the only bed in the house, to sleep a while, and then showed us the shower. She handed us the one pair of family shower slippers to wear. While Ana Maria and I took turns resting and showering in the yellow slippers, she sent a neighbor girl to get something special for breakfast. The girl returned holding two eggs and four small rolls in a cloth. In the ceremony with which we were given egg and bread around the tiny kitchen table, I realized that we were being honored with a special meal.

René and Ricardo, his brother, called the airline to find out the next flight to Jaqué, which was in two days. We made reservations over the phone, but we had to purchase the tickets at the counter, so we headed off to the airline office with the boys as our guides. I also wanted to buy a dictionary because I was having a problem understanding quite a few things.

Ana Maria said that it wasn't my Spanish that was the problem but the difference in words from region to region. Certain words kept tripping me up, such as *la baina,* which I had already heard a few times; it roughly translated to "thing" and was used in as wide a manner. The word had a bit of a double meaning, though, depending on the situation and intonation. Two very innocent words I had learned as some of my first in Spanish also had a wicked side. *Comer,* the word for "to eat" and *tirar,* the word for "to throw" had double meanings here. Ana Maria had begun to translate from the regional vocabulary into the Spanish with which I was familiar.

After hearing me struggle with Spanish in my conversations with René and a few other men along the way, Ana Maria gave me some advice. "Your accent is so good," she said, "that people will think you understand everything. And you are always nodding your head 'Yes,' and saying '*Sí,*' even when you don't understand. Believe me, that can be dangerous, especially with these Latin men," she laughed. "So when you don't understand, you have to say '*No,*' not '*Sí.*' *Comprende?*"

4

WITH RENÉ AND Ricardo as our guides, Ana Maria and I took a taxi to the city center. The streets of Panama City were filled with Christmas lights, decorations, and people moving madly from place to place. I had thought I might escape the pre-Christmas craze which is so much a part of the season at home, but here it was, full force—lights blinking on and off, neon signs, houses and stores decorated to capacity, everywhere a sign pleading purchase. Styrofoam Santas and plastic Nativity scenes stood in front of several houses and shops. The artificial trees were both familiar and strange, trimmed with animal masks and Panamanian flutes hanging alongside sleighs and flying reindeer.

There were many such odd marriages: ramshackle houses boasting the fanciest of lights and blinking icons. The old part of the city had magnificent buildings that spoke of a wealthy past but were now in complete disrepair. Many had several small gouges that Ricardo identified as bullet holes. We stopped in traffic in front of one such building, which bore a sign cautioning that it could come tumbling down at any moment. As I pointed it out to Ana Maria, a small child walked out onto the balcony, saw us looking, and waved.

There was a gathering of demonstrators which made our driver turn down a different road, cursing. I saw a few people with signs in their hands which said: *"Bases Militares, NO!"* The taximan was not very forthcoming about the demonstration. I stopped asking him questions when another woman walked by carrying a sign which read: *"Ni mineros ni gringeros"* (neither mines nor gringos). René said he didn't know much about this particular demonstration but that there had been quite a few student protests against American military bases and mining companies recently. "I suppose the holiday season is a good time to protest," he said. "The people are all out in the streets shopping anyway. You don't have to bring them out of their homes."

"Actually," Ricardo added, "It's more like people have wised up to the way the government works. In the past, the government has made a lot of major controversial decisions during holidays, when the people are too involved with their families to get political. Or too drunk."

The lack of traffic lights made the streets hard to navigate. The cars challenged one another at every street corner, narrowly avoiding accident after accident. Shouts and shaken fists would follow. This was traffic at its most raw, leaving it up to the drivers to force a way through the intersections.

The streets were congested, the smog level high. Strung on poles over one crossing was a set of Christmas lights spelling out *"Oxígeno Oxígeno"* in bold display. No one could explain the message. The buses were richly decorated with figures from saints to cartoons; several—and perhaps it was the season— had religious themes. A purple Jesus of Nazareth bus nearly ran us down.

It was a tradition to paint the buses for good luck, to give each a name and an identity. It reminded me of something I had seen a year before in Copacabana, along Lake Titicaca in Bolivia, a place famous for the blessing of buses. People thronged there from all over Peru and Bolivia to have their buses blessed by the *Virgen de Copacabana*. I had been given the honor by a bus driver first to drink a glass of champagne and then throw another on the front of the bus. It is no wonder the buses needed blessing, given the kind of driving I had witnessed. At least here in the city, one couldn't fall off the side of a mountain, as had been the danger in the Andes, with one bus challenging another on a road just wide enough for one, along a rocky cliffside with a plunge of several hundred yards—if one should fall.

5

WE COULDN'T LEAVE Panama City without seeing the canal that had given it such notoriety. We contacted Germán Torres, a friend of a friend of Ana Maria, who swept us up within the hour. Germán took us out for the afternoon to give us a small tour of the locks of the canal. We stopped first at Miraflores Locks, where a ship was passing through, being lifted and lowered through the system of locks. *Miraflores* means "see flowers," and I asked Germán where the name came from. He said the area used to be rich with flowers all year round. Now it is rich in tourists. No flowers.

It is the same story everywhere. I have often driven through the suburbs of Miami, wincing at the names given to new developments: Cypress Hammocks, Mangrove Estates, Sawgrass Mills Mall. Every few weeks a new project would be visible from the Sawgrass Expressway. Names are all that remain of the landscape that has been paved over, names that only signify what used to live there. In its place, an artificial landscape now exists. Developers dig huge holes to provide drainage and call them "lakes" to sell "waterfront property." Every morning back home I would run by Everglades School, miles and miles away from any Everglades, and think about the changing landscape, shifting with every step I took.

The Panama Canal, by now, looked as though it had always been there, although I knew it was one of the first great feats of reshaping landscape the twentieth century had seen. Charles V of Spain proposed a canal as early as 1534, but it was beyond the technical capabilities of that time. But the Spanish did pave mule trails across the isthmus to carry tons of silver and gold back to Spain from the conquest of Peru and other lands. Remnants of *Las Cruces* (the trail of crosses) could still be seen.

The United States had a large hand in constructing the Panama Railroad, which was completed just in time to make a fortune for its North American owners, by carrying gold-seekers across the isthmus on their way to California. And fifty years later the United States took over the rights and equipment from a bankrupt French company to complete the great canal connecting the oceans. Suspicions of fraud surrounded the process.

After unsuccessful negotiations with Colombia regarding the Panama Canal, Nobel Peace Prize-winner Theodore Roosevelt decided that a Panamanian revolution was the most certain path to his goal of obtaining control of the canal from, as he wrote to Secretary of State John Hay, "those contemptible little creatures in Bogotá."[1] He queried John Hay as to whether the United States might "interfere . . . when it becomes necessary so as to secure the Panama route without further dealing with the foolish and homicidal corruptionists in Bogotá."[2] The major force behind the revolution, Roosevelt gloriously proclaimed in 1903, "I took the Canal Zone and let Congress debate."[3]

The Panama operation represented North American attitudes of the era. Latin America was considered by many Americans to be merely an appendage of the United States, another direction for the nation to pursue its Manifest Destiny. In the mid-nineteenth century, the filibusterer William Walker, working for bankers Morgan and Garrison, invaded Central America. He named himself President of El Salvador, Honduras, and Nicaragua and restored slavery in these regions. Walker was paraded as a hero in the States. In 1912, President William Taft declared:

The day is not far distant when three Stars and Stripes at three equidistant points will mark our territory: one at the North Pole, another at the Panama Canal, and the third at the South Pole. The whole hemisphere will be ours in fact as, by virtue of our superiority of race, it already is ours morally.[4]

Taft also noted that U.S. foreign policy "may well be made to include active intervention to secure for our merchandise and our capitalists opportunity for profitable investment."[5]

From London, Friedrich Engels wrote at the time: "The Panama business could well become for the bourgeois republic a Pandora's box, this grand National Steeplechase of Scandals. The miracle has been performed of transforming a canal which has not been dug out, into an unfathomable abyss."[6]

At the time of our visit, the canal zone was still sovereign U.S. territory leased from Panama. The presence of the United States in *La Zona* has shaped Panamanian society. The main unit of currency is the American dollar. The first Americans working at the canal were mostly from southern states, and they established a colonial system in the Zone. There were two pay scales established: one for the Americans (the gold scale) and another for the Panamanians (the silver scale). Despite the discrimination, many Panamanians flocked to take jobs in the Zone. Though the pay was inferior to the whites', it was higher than they could get in the rest of Panama. They could shop in the Zone commissaries, and their children went to special schools (separate from North Americans, however). These *Zonistas* formed their own distinct society, neither Panamanian nor American. The next generations, especially, have had a great deal of trouble fitting in with the rest of Panamanian society.

The Panama Canal is fifty miles long from the Atlantic to the Pacific. It was cut through a low, narrow saddle of the long mountainous isthmus that joins North and South America. The canal's principal features are Gatun Lake, the man-made lake stretching across the isthmus; Gaillard Cut, the excavation through the Continental Divide that extends the lake to Pedro

Miguel Locks; the Gatun, Pedro Miguel, and Miraflores Locks that raise the ships between sea level and the lake; and the ports of Balboa on the Pacific and Cristobal on the Atlantic.

At the time the canal was built, in the first decade of the 1900s, Gatun Dam was the largest earth dam that had ever been constructed, and Gatun Lake was the largest man-made lake in the world. The three sets of locks were the most massive concrete structures ever built.

Coming from the Atlantic, a ship enters the Gaillard Cut, once called the Culebra (Snake) Cut, and passes Gold Hill on the left, which rises 662 feet above sea level. Contractor's Hill, on the West Bank, used to have an altitude of 410 feet, but this was reduced to 370 to stabilize the hill. Various portions of the cut have been widened over the years. The Pacific-bound ship first enters Gatun Locks where it is raised 78 feet to the level of Gatun Lake. At the other end of the lake, it goes through Pedro Miguel Locks and is lowered thirty-one feet in one step to Miraflores Lake, a small artificial body of water a mile wide that separates Pedro Miguel and Miraflores Locks. The ship is then lowered the remaining two steps to Pacific sea level at Miraflores Locks, which is slightly over a mile in length. The lock gates at Miraflores are the tallest of any in the system because of the extreme tidal variations of the Pacific Ocean.

Altogether, ships transiting the canal are raised and lowered eighty-five feet through the mountain from sea level to sea level.

The transfer of control of the canal from the United States to Panama on December 31, 1999, was preceded by negotiations that brought to the surface a number of environmental issues. The canal itself is endangered by the loss of forests and wetlands surrounding it. Rainfall provides much of the water necessary to operate the locks. The forested areas around the waterway allow the water to flow cleanly. If the forests are cleared, the soil will no longer be anchored by the trees' roots, and then the silt washing down could block the canal and cause many problems. The *El Niño* (the warming of tropical Pacific waters) of the late 1990s caused a severe drought in the area, making the canal impassable for many larger ships. The canal watershed is also a main source of drinking water for the nation's 2.5 million people.

The process of closing the U.S. military's Panama bases, in compliance with the 1977 treaty, was long and complex. Among other problems, the negotiations between the United States and Panama over the handover produced a major dispute about the cleanup of toxics, munitions, and other environmental hazards. Firing and bombing ranges were a major concern to the Panamanians, but the United States feared setting a precedent for other countries where bases may be removed. Forty percent of the former ranges are in protected watersheds that have flora and fauna unknown anywhere else in the world. Many of the "protected" areas will be very difficult to clean up as they have unexploded bombs beneath them.

German pointed out the Bridge of the Americas, its dark silhouette rising 384 feet above the ocean. We had driven over it the night before, when we arrived in the city on the bus. Ana Maria had shaken me and pointed out the breathtaking view of the ribbon of water below us, opening out into the Pacific. The bridge reunited land divided during construction of the canal and formed another link in the Panamerican Highway.

The Panamerican Highway commences in Fairbanks, Alaska, and extends down through Canada and the western United States, then crosses into Mexico and continues through Guatemala, El Salvador, Honduras, Nicaragua, Costa Rica, to the center of Panama at Yavisa. There it stops abruptly at a virtual wall of dense forest. The highway resurfaces again about a hundred kilometers farther on in Colombia and plunges down through Ecuador and Peru, ending at the southern tip of Chile.

The Darién Gap is the short stretch through the Darién region of Panama and Chocó region of Colombia, where the road breaks. For years, there has been a great deal of debate and controversy about the completion of the Panamerican Highway through the Darién region. The indigenous people believe that construction will have a disastrous effect on the environment and on the preservation of their cultures. It will bring the First World directly into their villages. The complex and delicate balance of a rain-forest ecosystem clearly shows that one cannot simply lay a road through the forest. It affects everything around it.

Germán told us about some of the controversy surrounding the Panamerican Highway from his perspective. "I am Emberá," he said, "even though I have spent many years in the city. I know what this road will do to my people in the forest. The old ways of the forest will be completely lost. There will be nothing left. Only cities. The traditional life of the Emberá *is* the forest. I speak from three perspectives," he added. "I am Emberá, African, and European."

"As is the case of much of your country," I said.

"No, not really, because much of the country is mixed, but who really knows what they are? I know the three distinct lines," he tapped his chest.

I thought about what he said, how he almost denied being mixed because he could trace and name his roots, unlike so many people in the New World. It was almost as though it made him a first generation, in a sense, the point at which the rivers converged.

As I stood with Germán, watching a ship going up and over the mountain, I had a strong sense of the power of this thin ribbon of connecting land that we had snipped through from ocean to ocean. I envisioned the travel that had taken place for millennia, prehistoric men and women migrating through Central America to settle in South America, probably as early as 8000 B.C. I could see the ghost ship of Columbus, which would cause such great change in such short time.

I thought about the "independence" of Panama and of how much the history of the region depended on the fact of its thin geography, perfect for carving a waterway to hasten the transport of people, gold, oil, and countless other resources in the New World. As Eduardo Galeano noted in *Memory of Fire,* "no one mentions the Antillean, Chinese, and East Indian workers whom yellow fever and malaria have exterminated at the rate of seven hundred dead per kilometer of canal opened through the mountains."[7]

U. S. intervention in Panama has continued into recent years with events such as the invasion of Panama in 1989 to overthrow Noriega. The invasion was carried out in the name of fighting the drug war, although a popular belief in Panama is that the overthrow was inspired by Noriega's knowledge of President Bush's involvement in covert operations in Latin America.

I asked Germán where he had been during the invasion, and he said matter-of-factly, "Right in town. I stayed inside, though, and watched the Americans go by. I know when to stay inside. Did you notice all the holes in the buildings when you drove through town. What do you think they're from?"

He paused and then continued, "It was a terrible time. It's one of the reasons there is so much student demonstration these days to get Americans out of the country."

I said we had seen part of the protest from the cab earlier that day. "I took a picture," I told him, "of several people carrying a banner with the words *"Mr. Clinton, Bases Militares, NO! Olvidar Jamás! (Never forget)."*

"The picture should be a good one," I added, "since they were assembled directly in front of the McDonald's."

As we left the canal, we passed a sign indicating two towns in opposite directions: Diablo (Devil) was one way; Paraiso (Paradise) was on the other side.

I pointed it out to Ana Maria, who said, "Heaven and Hell are probably much closer than that. When you are flying in Paradise, you are probably always in danger of dropping below to singe your wings. If there is a Heaven and a Hell, they are probably closely bordering each other or possibly on either side of a river. Jurado is like that. Heaven on one side. Hell on the other." She was referring to the little town on the edge of the Colombian rain forest to which we were heading.

Germán, driving, turned his head from the road and said, "Actually, the people of Diablo have been seriously considering changing the name of their town."

6

THAT NIGHT WE went to Restaurante La Cascada (Restaurant of the Waterfall). At the restaurant's entrance, statues of mermaids and fish greeted us, and more of the same decorated the walls on the way in, along with stuffed lizards, deer, and bats. The canopies over the tables were covered with flowers, and hanging over the center of each table was a large electronic device with a red light that, at first, puzzled me.

The menu was sixteen pages long, translated into a peculiar English at the bottom of each page. I was hooked by the first line:

> Gentlemen, Now you are in the bigest restaurant in Panama that you have heard so much about. You are also looking at a very big menu but please do not get frighten or desilusioned because it is not as big as it looks because besides the food of the menu it also contains:
>
> A. Literature of the Cascade (Page No. 15)
> B. Philosophic phrases of the Cascade (Page No. 16)

C. Explications, Inventions, Secrets, Recipes (Pages No. 2-4)

D. Guide and Curious Informations for those who have come for the first time. (Page No. 5)

A note at the bottom of page 14 explained the red lights:

> In case you have not noticed yet, The Cascade has invented an electronic system, so that the customer can call the waitresses every time he needs her. That is why every time you want to call her, simply turn on the red bulb by turning the switch which is at the end of your table or hanging over your table because this switch lights up the red bulb that is at the end of your table or over your table, and also lights another bulb which is on the column next to the cashier and supervisor plus another bulb which is in the kitchen, with this system of call your waitresses is at your table in seconds.

And page 15 included seventeen points about the Cascade, including these highlights:

> 2. Because it has been created out in the free air and with natural plants, flowers, petrified animals, birds and fishes. . . .
>
> 4. A torrent of crystal-clear water bathing the giant cascade and cooling and refreshing the ornaments of the huge aquarium.
>
> 5. "The Cascade" is like an oasis, is like a dream, is like a fantasy, is like a mini disneyland in Panama. . . .
>
> 15. "The Cascade" is ideal to go by yourself to rest, to relax . . . having as a roof the sky, the stars and the moon and be caressed by the many colorfull plants and flowers, and having as companios the petrified animals, birds, and fishes which are serving some as fountains. . . .
>
> 17. Dear Panamanian, the creation of "The Cascade"

means a lot of faith and love for Panama, please
the care of her and feel proud because many
tourists will admire her and when they return
home they will talk about her, and their wonderful
stories will inspire other tourists to visit Panama,
more tourists, more progress and "The Cascade"
restaurant is ideal to suggest and recoment to
tourists, visitors and all americans because
all those people love, enjoy and admire "The
Cascade" and all these people are people who
save their money on their countries to come here
and spend it in our country, and that is why we all
have an obligation and we owe it to them to try
hard to make them happy. So God bless our
tourists, our visitors and all the americans.

At the bottom of page 15, it said, "If you want to take home our menu please look page No. 12 and paragraph #A." I had already decided I must have one, so I located the appropriate paragraph:

If you like any page or all the pages of our menu, they
are free, just help yourself, they are in the table in front
of the cashier next to the aquarium.

Now, if you like to have the whole menu in plastic,
total of 16 pages please pay the cashier $3.00 and ask
for your receipt to show on the way out.

7

What the people of the city do not realize is that the roots of all living things are interconnected. When a mighty tree is felled, a star falls from the sky.

— Chan K'in, Lacandon Mayan patriarch

Before we left the city, we attended a meeting that Hector Huertas Gonzalez, a Cuna lawyer who worked for the indigenous people of Panama, had set up with the Coordinadora Nacional de Pueblos Indigenas de Panama (COONAPIP; National Coordinator of Indigenous Communities of Panama). There were representatives from the five different indigenous peoples in Panama: Ngobe-Bugle, Cuna, Naso, Emberá, and Wounaan (in Panama, the last two tribes are often united and live in the same community and thus are referred to as Emberá-Wounaan). They were gathering to discuss the current issues facing each and all of their communities. The main issues to be discussed were the Panamerican Highway and other roads, military bases, research facilities, and mining concessions being given by the government to international companies on indigenous land.

The Cuna people are the best organized of the indigenous people of Panama. The meeting began with a Cuna representative relating a recent incident regarding the presence of the

Smithsonian Institution on Cuna land. The Smithsonian has had a significant presence in Panama. Its tropical research center is located here; Panamanian scientists work at the center but are often not treated collegially by the Americans. The colonial mentality has actually resulted in one of the center's facilities (located on a Cuna island) being closed down by the Cuna.

"We were unhappy with the facility because the scientists would not let us know what they were doing," the representative said. "When they decided to illuminate the coral reef at night without explaining why to the people, some of the light bulbs they had brought over 'disappeared.' The response of the institute was the final insult. They organized a search party and went through our village on a hut-to-hut search. That was the end. We demanded they remove their facility."

The Smithsonian Tropical Research Center director, savvy in American politics, had believed all would run smoothly with the institute because he had secured the approval of the Cuna chiefs. He had paid the rent directly to them. This, however, is not the way Cuna society functions. It is extremely democratic. Village affairs are conducted in daily meetings in which all the residents participate. Tribal affairs are governed by periodic general councils where thousands of people participate, not merely the chiefs. The Cuna people expect to be informed about and actively participate in the decision-making. Chiefs are not above criticism. In fact, an established practice during council is for the chief to sit on a low stool in the center of the room. Any tribe member can walk up to him and tell him, in front of the entire assembly, what it is they do not like about him or the decisions he has made.

A representative from a Ngobe-Bugle village then spoke at length about mining concessions. He said that sixty-four exploration concessions had recently been given to American and Canadian companies such as Geomina. He spoke of the 1958 legal statute that gives the indigenous people the right to the land in question. The catch, however, is the same all over South America: the indigenous peoples have land rights but not mineral rights. They do not own those things the multinationals feel have value. According to the government, they do not have rights to what lies beneath the land. The government retains the right to allow companies to enter this land for mining activity.

The Cuna representative spoke about recent dealings with the president of Panama regarding mineral rights. President Balladares had proposed to sell mineral rights to Cuna land, and the Cuna had responded by banning him from their lands. The response from the government had been that "the Cuna are mistaken if they think they are a separate government." The conflict had escalated, and in an effort to keep peace, the president had sent a minister to the Cuna. The Cuna refused to receive the minister; they refused to receive anyone except Balladares himself. The president finally did visit the tribe, and the proposal regarding the mineral rights was "shelved."

The people fear what mining will do to their lands. They have seen the contamination of the rivers, the deforestation, the erosion of the topsoil, the eradication of plant and animal life, the building of roads through virgin forest to bring machinery in and ores out. The mining roads also open access to poachers and settlers. The Cuna have organized marches and hunger strikes to protest the government concessions.

It is often hard to identify the corporations responsible for the damage, since exploration companies often obtain the rights and then sell them to other companies. It is an expanding and lucrative business, but at the expense of the indigenous communities. As a Ngobe-Bugle representative Marcelino Montezuma said, "We have been struggling for our rights for five hundred years. We have been exploited by all manner of companies as laborers on banana and coffee plantations. We have never been paid what we should be paid. Each family of the Ngobe-Bugle has about two acres' allotment. The landowners and cattlemen have about a thousand acres each. One cow has more land than we do."

In Panama, there is land referred to as *tierras baldias* (land without owner), which Irenare, an environmental protection agency, is assigned to "protect." But the people at the meeting were angry at Irenare's statement that indigenous people are not capable of protecting the land. One remark summed up the general sentiment: "It is thanks to us that these places still exist."

The *cacique* (chief) of one of the Emberá-Wounaan communities, Facundo Sancho, spoke about Irenare and the recent attempt to keep the indigenous people from cutting wood and killing animals. This question is being raised in so many parts of the world. Industrial society, which has affected ecosystems so dramatically with such actions as large-scale mining and harvesting of trees, now begins imposing laws that outlaw the taking of a tree to build a canoe or the hunting of animals for food. The self-sustainability of the people is being systematically undermined. There are forty Emberá-Wounaan communities inside *comarcas* (reservations) and forty outside. The government, however, has created national parks within the comarcas without consulting the indigenous populations who live there. The spokespersons considered this a serious insult and were very vocal about their anger.

The Cuna representatives were equally vocal. "We practice agroforestry," one man stood and said. "We did so long before the research institutes came up with the word. We don't clear-cut. We plant in between the trees—coconuts, bananas, our medicinal plants. We have always planted under the canopy and chosen trees to cut very carefully. And now the government is pushing these laws which will make our very way of life against the law."

Several people voiced concern about the Panamerican Highway, the completion of which has been in debate for many years. Government proposals had again been floated to extend the road past Yavisa, through the Panamanian Darién and Colombian Chocó. The road through Darién would cross Emberá land. Facundo Sancho said, "If they create the road, that will be the end of our people."

Impact assessments have clearly shown the disastrous effect such a road would have on the ecosystem and on traditional life. The people also logically fear the guerrillas and narco-traffic that would probably then pass through their lands. Some comments were made about requesting legal rights to territory around the portion of the highway already constructed from Panama City to Yavisa. The people spoke about being in favor of improvements on that section of highway but not of extending it any further. "Development, for us, is not to destroy the land," one speaker said.

The native peoples are wary of the large inter-American development banks and the World Bank, which fund roads and other projects. They are also wary of associations such as Irenare, which perform certain impact assessments that the indigenous people feel might well be slanted, because the government has a hand in Irenare. The comment was made that "organizations which protect the environment must take into consideration the reality of the indigenous peoples' ways of life." They also believe the studies should be performed by their own indigenous representatives.

This demand is quite valid, as no one has more or better knowledge about how to utilize the environment sustainably than the indigenous peoples. The ecological wisdom of indigenous peoples has been recognized in the 1987 Brundtland report of the World Commission on Environment and Development:

> Their very survival has depended upon their ecological awareness and adaptation. . . . These communities are the repositories of vast accumulations of traditional knowledge and experience that links humanity with its ancient origins. Their disappearance is a loss for the larger society, which could learn a great deal from their traditional skills in sustainably managing very complex ecological systems. It is a terrible irony that as formal development reaches more deeply into rainforests, deserts, and other isolated environments, it tends to destroy the only cultures that have proved able to thrive in these environments.[1]

One would think our actions would reflect such bold recognition, but policy is a slow-moving beast. The people here were well aware of the workings of bureaucracy and the time it takes to reverse the destruction that is called progress. They spoke strongly in support of coalitions and solidarity between all indigenous communities regarding mining and roads. At the close of the meeting, they brought up concerns about indigenous knowledge, such as traditional medicine, referring to it as intellectual property, a term and concept that clearly come from the Western world.

In many regions around the world, traditional knowledge has been exploited and stolen in the same way that lands were invaded and religions were destroyed. The people feel they should be compensated for what modern science has learned from them.

We are only now recognizing the vast medicinal potential of areas such as the South American rain forests. And communities such as the Emberá are rightfully wary of revealing any more knowledge in return for nothing. David Suzuki's and Peter Knudtson's book, *Wisdom of the Elders*, recognizes the potent, many-layered nature of native knowledge:

> Native knowledge and spiritual values are not simply "natural resources" (in this case intellectual ones) for non-Natives to mine, manipulate or plunder. They are, and will always be, the precious life-sustaining property of First Peoples: sacred symbols encoding the hidden design of their respective universes; mirrors to their individual and collective identities; and ancient and irreplaceable maps suggesting possible paths to inner as well as ecological equilibrium with the wider, ever-changing world.[2]

There has been a disappearance of forests and cultures around the world, from the gray rocky hills around the Mediterranean, which used to be rich with groves and wildlife, to the lowland hardwood forests of China, which were mostly gone by about thirty-five hundred years ago, to the United States, with the mining and clear-cutting that have altered the landscape from the Pacific redwood forests to the Gulf Stream waters. The word "desertification" means nothing to most of us, though we have created deserts all over the world—and will create more if fears about global warming prove true. With modern industrial capacity, the pace has quickened over the centuries, and the rate of destruction has multiplied to alarming proportions.

In Cuna legend, the Earth-Mother gives birth to a bar of gold. But the people speak of gold as more than just the precious metal: it is the earth's fruits and vegetables, all life. The golden frog heals the tree of life. The tree reaches into the sky, where there is an island of trees, at the top of which there is a large pot of *chicha* which is always full. The tree represents the link between earth and sky, man and woman, the interconnecting web of all life.

My notebooks are filled with the names of trees and the stories that surround them. The oak tree was sacred to the Druids, as was the fig tree of Romulus to the Romans, and it was under the Bodhi tree that the Buddha attained enlightenment. In alchemy, the Tree of Knowledge is called *arbor philosophica,* a symbol of evolution or the development of an idea. To plant the philosopher's tree means to stimulate creative energy.

The fig tree has also been a Christian symbol, and in fact, Christian symbolism is full of depictions of the tree as an axis linking different worlds. A duality exists in the symbolism of trees in the Bible. Both the Tree of Life and the Tree of Knowledge of Good and Evil were centrally placed in the Garden, but the Tree of Life was perhaps hidden, like the secret of immortality. Perhaps it was hidden until such time as humans might recognize its existence.

The Cuna and the Emberá and other indigenous people, particularly in South America, have versions of the same myth about the Tree of Life, which bore all food plants. In some versions, it was filled with fish, which were killed. In all versions, the tree was felled, and in its trunk was water, which flooded the world.

As we left the COONAPIP meeting, I thought back to that day with Germán, seeing the silhouette of the Bridge of the

Americas like some animal caught in a great leap, reconnecting the land divided by the canal. It was new, yet it reminded me of the bridges I crossed every day as a child. My hometown of Miami Beach was all bridges, connecting island to island to island—man-made or natural. Somehow those bridges had directed me south across vaster ones, and now I was to cross this land bridge between the continents and reach the other ocean.

I wanted to see the unimaginable trees that still grew in the rain forest, stretching wider than houses and towering skyward. The Cuna story made me think of the Cherokee myth my grandmother had told me years ago, of the earth as a great island floating in a great sea. "When the earth grows old and worn out, it will sink down and all will be water again."

We were at the seashore when she told me this. Our backs were to the city—as each wave rolled in that night, having traveled all that distance across the world only to roll out again.

TWO

La Frontera

*As the waiting of the eels off the mouth of the bay
was only an interlude in a long life filled with constant
change, so the relation of sea and coast and mountain
ranges was that of a moment of geologic time. For
once more the mountains would be worn away by the
endless erosion of water and carried in silt to the sea,
and once more all the coast would be water again, and
the places of its cities and towns would belong to
the sea.*

—RACHEL CARSON,
Under the Sea Wind

8

We left Panama City the next morning on a tiny plane which would make a stop in Jaqué. There was a dirt road to Jaqué, but it was so bad that it could take days to travel it. The plane had just arrived at the tiny terminal, and people were climbing down the stairs of the aircraft, while a few attendants formed piles of luggage for passengers arriving and for those leaving. A slight rain was falling. I watched our bags of books join a pile of cardboard-box luggage, probably full of goods purchased in Panama City to take back to Jaqué. It looked as though every-thing would be wet by the time they had finished loading. The plane needed a coat of paint and seemed a bit rickety. It did not inspire total confidence.

German met us at the airport with his brother Heriberto, who had an envelope in his hand for Jaime Torres, a third brother, who was the director of the school in Jaqué and had a guesthouse there. He said it was a birthday letter for Jaime. Right before the plane left, Heriberto came running up to me with a five-dollar bill to add to the envelope for Jaime.

German also put a poem in my hand that he had recited the other day and that I had asked him to transcribe:

La rosa tembloroza se desprendio del tallo
y la arrastro la briza hacia
las aguas turbias del pantano

Flotaron sobre el agua sus petalo mutilados
y confudidos con el lodo negro
mas negros (que) el lodo negro se tornaron.

Pero en las noches puras y serenas se sentia
vagar por el espacio un leve olor a rosas
en las aguas turbias del pantano

> *The tremulous rose fell off the stem*
> *and the breeze whisked it*
> *to the turbid waters of the marsh*

> *Her broken petals floated on the water*
> *and mixed with the dark mud*
> *growing darker*

> *But in the nights, pure and serene*
> *the slight scent of roses wanders*
> *in the turbid waters of the marsh*

René and Ricardo also came to bid us a good journey. We had acquired a large family in our few days in Panama City.

We were told there was a weight limit for the plane, and we were far over it, with all the books and microscopes. Ana Maria suddenly turned on the charm. I was getting used to it by then. She had the manner of a tough woman on a mission, but she was also a very attractive young woman and had learned how this can be used to one's advantage, particularly here, where it seemed an expected part of the transaction.

I thought back to our border crossing from Costa Rica to Panama, when we discovered we needed a visa for Panama. Getting one issued at the border could take a few days. The office was closed, but Ana Maria fluttered her eyes—she really did flutter her eyes—at the guards, who finally found someone to issue us visas. When we were in the office, he said he couldn't do them that night, but Ana Maria knew the local rules well. She had told me before that money could get us out of certain troubles, but tears would also work very well—and were cheaper. Within moments, she had tears streaming down her face, her voice breaking, telling a story about the need for our hurry, how we wanted to make it to Chocó by Christmas, and a moment later, the guard was helplessly issuing us visas.

So I wasn't very surprised when, in response to Ana Maria's outpouring of despair over our inability to pay any overweight charges, they waived the extra fee.

After having all of our personal belongings hand-searched and having to explain the purpose of the microscopes, we boarded the plane. It had about twenty seats and was almost full. The locals had immediately taken the windows, but learning quickly, I grabbed the last one. Ana Maria squeezed in beside me. The upholstery on the seats was torn in places, and as I pointed to the exposed foam rubber with a worried face, Ana Maria laughed. "You have to give yourself over—or else get off the plane," she said.

After fantasizing a moment about getting off the plane and heading home on the next real airline, I decided to stay put. I tried to focus on the scene around me.

As the last of the people boarded, along with a prize rooster in a cage and a small dog in a basket, the captain wove down the aisle through the passengers, stepped off the plane for a moment, and then reboarded and made his way back to the cockpit. The doors were closed behind him. Within minutes, we were off down the runway, the engine screaming in my ears, blocking out the screams inside my head, and then suddenly we were in the air, flying steadily. Given our successful takeoff and the relative calm of the other passengers, I loosened my grip on Ana Maria's arm.

The flight took less than an hour, but people immediately

began dragging out their lunches. The smell of cheese and bananas wafted over. An older woman on the other side of Ana Maria offered us some bread, which Ana Maria accepted for us.

"Never refuse bread," she said to me, smiling at the woman.

The plane had a rather low altitude, which made me somewhat nervous, and I looked out of the window at the landscape below. The rain had nearly stopped, but small droplets still slid down the windows. We were just a few minutes from the city, but everything below us had become green. I could see narrow roads running through the countryside. I felt a mixed sense of relief at being out of the city and nervousness about what was to come. I watched as the landscape become more and more wild below us.

The wilderness was broken as we passed over a huge square cut out of the forest. "Look at that," I showed Ana Maria.

"It's useful that we're coming by plane," she said, shaking her head, "because you can really see the damage this way."

As we flew on, the bare patches in the landscape became more frequent. It looked as if the forest had been gouged out in many places. "This is all in the last few years," Ana Maria said, "and it's worse in Colombia."

The woman in front of me was staring over her husband out of the window. "Look at the holes," I overheard her say.

"The what?" he answered.

"The cutting," she pointed below.

He looked out the window again and said, "It looks pretty bad from up here," he said. "But it's good money. And there are plenty of trees. I mean, it's not like we're going to run out of trees."

I looked over at Ana Maria, but she hadn't heard—the engine was too loud. I didn't say anything, just turned my head back to the window, pressed my forehead against it, and watched the patchwork of land pass under us.

9

We landed on a dirt runway with a small hut that appeared to be the terminal. The plane was met by many curious villagers, including a large contingent of children, who rushed forward to carry our bags. We asked for the Torres house, and the parade of children took us down a dirt road which they said ended at the beach. We could feel all eyes on us as we walked the mile or so. The people we passed all had dark skin, but their faces showed a mix of indigenous and European ancestry. Ana Maria had told me that the people were mostly descendants of Africans who had fled enslavement years ago, reached the Pacific ocean, and could go no further. Some had come by boat along the coast from Colombia.

When we arrived at the Torres house, we met Germán's brother, Jaime. He bore a striking resemblance to Germán, although he was somewhat darker-skinned and had lighter eyes which lit up his face. I gave him the letter from Heriberto and wished him a happy birthday. He seemed somewhat stunned at the unexpected, unlikely visitors, but he quickly became the good host, offered us a room, and asked us how long we were staying.

The Torres "hotel" was still in the process of being completed. The rooms had been built one floor up in case of high water, and underneath the house, three hammocks were swaying slightly in the breeze. Jaime proudly pointed out the indoor facilities—a toilet above a deep hole and the bath, which was a large tub of rainwater and a small bucket for scooping. Wood walls divided the bedrooms from each other, and we could hear even a whisper or a mosquito through them. The house was the closest structure to the ocean, and from the rooms, we could also hear the waves rolling in. We had a clear view of several huge rocks jutting out of the ocean. I pointed them out, and Jaime called them "Los Tres Reyes Magos" (the three wise men), but then said that was just a *sobrenombre* (nickname). They were really known as the three peaks of Jaqué.

Jaime had been on his way out when we arrived and had to leave, but he invited us to a bonfire on the beach that night. We put our things in our little room and went to investigate the boat situation. We knew that a boat would come to Jaqué a few times a week to bring passengers along the Pacific to Jurado, in Colombia, and to some of the neighboring villages. But apparently we had just missed the boat that afternoon, which meant that we had to stay in Jaqué for a few days. There was no other choice. So we went to register our arrival with the police, as was required.

It was about lunchtime, and the relief officer on duty was a shy young man, probably no older than eighteen, who merely recorded our passport numbers and the purpose of our visit, which, to keep matters simple, we just stated as *turismo*. He told us to be sure to return to the office to sign out when the next boat came. "The police chief will be sorry he missed you two," he said. We decided not to inquire further.

When we returned to the house on the beach, we found some of the children surfing with small wooden canoes. They invited us to try, but the canoe was incredibly unsteady, and I kept tipping it over before the wave even came. They reminded me of pirogues I had encountered a few years before in the bayous of Louisiana, one-person canoes that were dangerously unstable. I had paddled one down an alligator-filled bayou one afternoon, feeling alligators bump the boat from underneath, and had never forgotten the experience.

When I first put a leg into the boat, it tipped immediately, and all the children laughed out loud. Several pushed forward to give me advice.

"You have to use your hands to steady it."

"Swing both legs in at once."

Both legs in at once? What did they think I was—a monkey? Or probably just a lithe little twelve-year-old. After several awkward tries which inspired great laughter, I was finally able to squat in the boat without capsizing. I waited to catch a big wave that I saw rolling in from the distance. The moment the wave hit the boat, though, I was back in the water, this time with the canoe on top of me. I had three or four near-drownings. There was nothing the children could tell me, really. It was just a matter of getting used to the balance.

When I finally caught a wave, it was all the more glorious for the struggle. Once I was within the current of the wave, it seemed to take over the boat, and I rode on top of it all the way to shore. I never did stand up completely but figured I would leave that feat to the little experts—who were cheering my accomplishment as I came in.

"That was a big one!" one said.

"You want to catch another?"

I did, but it was getting late, and I decided to quit while I was ahead. I left the cool water exhilarated and joined Ana Maria and some of the children on the beach. She was drawing a story in the sand for them, walking down the beach making hieroglyphs: a boat and a dolphin and something that looked like an angel in the sand. She handed the stick to one of the children to add to the story. The child drew the moon and several lines she called waves. Ana Maria said the drawings were a poem one little boy had told, and she asked him to recite it again. I asked him his name, and he straightened up, tapped his chest and said, "Jorge Enrique Cordoba. 'Te Fuiste Marinerito,' por José Figuereda." He had learned the poem in school:

TE FUISTE MARINERITO

Te Fuiste Marinerito
En una noche lunada
Tan alegre, tan bonito
Cantando a la mar salada.

Cinco delfines remeros,
Su barco le cortejaba.
Dos angeles marineros
Invisibles le guiaban.

Tan dulce era tu cantar
Hasta, que el aire se enojaba
Tendio las redes
Sobre su mar salada

Y pesco la luna llena
sobre su platera.

YOU WENT, LITTLE SAILOR

You went, little sailor
On a moon-filled night
Content, lovely,
Singing to the salty ocean.

Five dolphin rowers
Courted your ship.
Two angel sailors
invisibly led you.

So sweet was your song,
Until the wind grew angry,
stretched its net
Over the salty waves

And fished the full moon
From out of the silver.

It was almost sunset. The light was growing perfect for photographs, and I took out my camera and began taking pictures of Ana Maria and the children, the canoes, the village in the background. The children were very interested in the camera. Most had never seen one before. They wanted their pictures taken, and they also wanted to snap some themselves.

I let each of them take a photograph. The children on the beach were very serious about their compositions, and they told me afterwards everything they had tried to get in their pictures. The sun had been sinking lower and lower toward the three big rocks. One little girl, Suli, said she had taken the sun upside down so that it wouldn't go into the ocean and we could stay out longer.

But even as she said it and pointed to the three peaks with her finger, the sun was already slipping into the water. Jorge spoke up with another poem, "El Sol Queria Bañarse," which his teacher, Marco Morales, had written:

EL SOL QUERIA BAÑARSE

El sol queria bañarse
porque tenia calor.
Llevaba el calor por dentro
que le quitaba la razon.
La luna se lo advirtio
hacia caer la tarde
se tiro al mar, y se ahogo

Al ver que el pobre se ahogaba
Todo negro el mar se puso
Las estrellas lloraban
de la tristeza que les dio.
Y se les aparecio la luna y le dijo
asusteis que manana de mananita
saldra por otro rincon.

Y la manana siguiente, sonriente
el sol salio por otro rincon.
Las estrellas reian y lloraban
El cielo se puso alegre
El mar de gozo bailo
La luna muy serena
en su cuarto se quedo.

THE SUN WANTED TO BATHE

The sun wanted to bathe
because of the heat of the day.
He had taken the heat inside
and thrown away all reason.
The moon observed
that as it became later,
he was falling into the ocean and
would drown.

As the sun drowned,
the sea became dark.
and the stars cried
from the sadness it gave them.
But the moon rose and said
Do not fear, in the morning
he will rise on the other side.

And the next morning, smiling,
the sun rose on the other side.
The stars laughed and cried.
The sky was light.
The ocean danced.
The cool, calm moon
stayed in her bedroom.

I was struck by the recitation. These children actually had poems in their heads. I suppose I had expected nothing more than one finds in the States, where the poems most people have in their heads come from television commercials. Few American students can recite a single poem, but almost all can complete a jingle like: "Two all beef patties, special sauce. . . ."

10

As we walked up from the beach, one of the older children, Miguel, overheard Ana Maria and me talking about something, and he wanted to know what the problem was.

"Well," Ana Maria said, "the fact is that hundred-year-old trees just like this one," she pointed to a huge oak, "are being cut down to make things like toilet paper."

He looked incredulous. "Toilet paper? From trees?" For a moment, I thought he was just remarking on the senseless practice. Actually he was, indirectly, but he really did not believe that paper came from trees. "That's crazy," he said.

The moment made me think of a comment one of my freshmen students back home had made. During a class discussion about worldwide deforestation, the student had proclaimed, "Oh, this is all well and good, but I mean, it's not like we need plants to live."

Other class members told me later that my face had turned pale. A few other students turned to the first and said things like, "Have you heard of the food chain?" and "Do you want to breathe?" I remember pausing a moment and then using the student's statement as an example of how removed we all are from the source of things. Water comes out of the faucet, goes down the drain. We buy everything ready-made in packages from the supermarket.

I could understand how someone could think that. Why would a young person in the United States think otherwise? In our city lives, we have so little green, and almost all of that is ornamental. Miami, though greener than many cities, is a built landscape and carries with it all the aspects of living in the city, particularly an American city. It is a place of vast abundance and vast waste. Unfortunately, the two tend to coexist in our nation which "throws away its cars when the ashtrays are full."

And here, in Jaqué, with all this lush vegetation around us, Miguel kept insisting that toilet paper couldn't possibly come from trees. "They wouldn't cut a tree down to make toilet paper," he said.

I didn't blame him for disbelieving. It doesn't make sense to me either. As we went back and forth, and I said again, "Believe me, it's true," a little girl who was standing nearby, listening, looked over and piped up, "No, it isn't. It comes from Panama City."

11

We ate dinner at one of the two restaurants in town, Rosita's, a small wood shack with one long table where the owner, who had given it her name, served a single dish for each meal, which she cooked only if there were any guests. The procedure was to ask what there was to eat that day and then to alter it slightly. I learned quickly that every drink came with sugar and consequently with little ants floating on top. It was standard fare in Latin America, and I had begun to make a point of asking for everything without sugar. I noticed that Rosita kept her bag of sugar in the center of a bowl of water to keep the ants from taking it over. We ate rice, beans, and fried bananas, the usual meal, which was occasionally served with a small piece of fish.

We invited Miguel, who had been hanging around, to eat with us. He acted truly honored and went home to change. I was still wearing my bathing suit, a conservative one piece, with a pair of shorts. When Miguel came to meet us, he was wearing a clean shirt and had his hair combed neatly. He looked around and whispered to me to put my shirt on. To him, the meal was a ceremonious occasion. I put on my shirt.

Miguel was quite a character. He was known around town for his deeds and misdeeds and liked to tell stories (which some of the locals called lies). I told him he had a writer in him. During the few days we were in town, he told us his parents lived in Jurado. Then he changed it to Buenaventura. He said he needed enough money to get back there. We later found out that they lived in Jaqué, as did his grandmother, who was the one that finally let us in on the truth. Miguel said he had five siblings, then paused and said six: Jesus, Maria, Feneli, Rosita, Gilma, Lamaye. He counted them on his fingers, as if no one had ever asked him the question before.

Miguel had a quick mind that we thought could be put to good use at something other than a con game. But I could relate to the con. He wanted a way out. Underneath the stories, Miguel had not led an easy life. Before we left, he put in my hand a poem:

> Ha cocaso aprendi mi labor de colegial
> en el colegio fiscal en el barrio donde naci
> Era mi primaria completa del estado de mi ninez
> Los sentabamos de tres en una sola carpeta
> Yo creo que la palmeta la inventaron para mi
> de la vez que una rompi
> Me apoderaron mano de fierro
> y por ser tan mata perro
> a cocaso aprendi

> *This was the way I learned*
> *in the school in the town where I was born,*
> *in my childhood education*
> *where we sat three on a single bench.*
> *I believe they invented the stick for me,*
> *since one broke over me,*
> *and they gave me a hand of iron.*
> *To be as fierce as they:*
> *This is what I learned.*

47

Outside the restaurant after dinner, there were some women playing bingo by a small fire. We walked by them, and one woman waved her hand and called out to us to join them. The stakes were very small, but it was real money on the table. I don't like to gamble and had agreed just to be sociable, but I proceeded to win the first round. So we stayed for a second one, which I won as well, as I did the third. Ana Maria won the fourth.

We certainly couldn't leave then. After the second game, I had almost tried to lose. They called the numbers very quickly, and I almost missed a few anyway. But the women sitting next to me kept filling up my card when I accidentally missed a number.

Finally, to my great relief, we began losing, and, after a few more rounds, considered ourselves free. We wanted to go and see the dancing at the pre-Christmas celebration in the square—we could hear the music playing in the center of the village.

Some of the older children were practicing *cumbias,* dances of African origin, in which the man invites the woman to dance, offering her a handful of lighted candles which she holds upright in her hand while whirling around him. The smoke trailed behind as the bodies wove in and out of each other, skirts flaring, and candlelight blurring into streaks. The dancers had to keep a certain pace, for if they moved too fast, they might accidentally snuff the candles out.

One *cumbia* song made me laugh when I listened closely enough to understand the words:

> Tiene plata, Tiene plata
> Tiene plata, y no me la da.
> Jombe, Jombe, Jombe.
>
> Tiene plata, tiene plata
> y el, solito, se la gasta.
> Jombe, Jombe, Jombe.

He has money, he has money
He has money, and gives me none.
Jombe, Jombe, Jombe.

He has money, he has money.
and as usual, he spends it all.
Jombe, Jombe, Jombe.

Some of the older women were arriving from all over the village at the same time we did, and they began the *novenas* in honor of the coming of Christmas. I always have trouble making out the words in songs in any language, but I finally realized they were repeating the same lines over and over again:

SAN ANTONIO YA SERA

Cuál es el niño que dice Mama?
Por qué no enseñan que diga Papa?
Cuál es el niño que dice Papa?
Por qué no enseñan que diga Mama?
San Antonio, ya será.

SAN ANTONIO IS COMING

Who is the child who says Mother?
Why don't they teach him to say Father?
Who is the child who says Father?
Why don't they teach him to say Mother?
San Antonio, it will be.

The people sang the same verses at least ten times, switching back and forth between "Papa" and "Mama." Without any pause, they shifted into another song with only one line: *Juego a la Lata* (Play the tin can), which aptly described the motley band and their instruments. The people danced to the songs, clapped their hands, shook rainsticks, and beat on drums and anything else they might have brought. Nuns in habits partied alongside young girls dressed seductively for a night out.

We joined in the songs ourselves, until we remembered the bonfire Jaime Torres had promised us, and we left the gathering. On the way back, Ana Maria told me a story from the southwest of Colombia, of La Montañerita Cimarrona (the Wild Woman of the Forest).

As the story goes, in 1560, an Indian told Miguel de Soto that in the jungle there was a woman identical to his Mary. He said she blessed their gardens and the forest, and the Indians played their flutes and danced in her honor. The Indians carried De Soto there on their backs, as was the custom for Europeans. Almost at the edge of the Pacific, he found her carved into the rocks, in her arms El Niño Dios. De Soto had her cut down from the rock and moved her to Cali, but she disappeared one night and was found again in the jungle. The Spanish built a special guarded chapel for her and changed her name to Our Lady of Remedies, because of the miracles she was known to perform.

The last novena we heard floated after us as we left for the night:

> La Nochebuena se viene
> La Nochebuena se va
> y nosotros nos iremeos
> y no volveremos mas

> *Christmas Eve comes*
> *and Christmas Eve goes*
> *and we are leaving on a journey*
> *never to return*

12

THE TORRES FAMILY had the bonfire going when we came back to the house. The children had gathered branches from the beach and piled them as high as a hut for a spectacular blaze. The moon was growing—it would be a full moon for Christmas—and with the bonfire and the clear night, it was easy to see the way to the beach. Ana Maria had been introducing me to people as *una poeta*. I was at first surprised but then always pleased by the respect and genuine interest this almost always evoked. It meant something different to be a poet in Colombia, in Latin America. Pablo Neruda, Octavio Paz, and César Vallejo awoke such passion for love and a simultaneous fervor for politics and commanded an intense respect throughout Latin America. I thought about the children and the way they had spoken their poems with such pride.

Jaime introduced us to his brother, Mene, who he said was also a poet. Mene told me he had traveled around the world by boat as a "fishing specialist" and began listing the ports he had been to. But he had always wanted to return to Jaqué, he said. He always knew he would. Mene confessed to the charge of being a poet, but he said he would write his poems and then throw them into the fire.

Jaime said it was the truth. He had seen his brother cast the words into the flames. He gestured at the bonfire, which was shooting out sparks like small stars.

The Torres family was well known in Jaqué. Jaime said his brother Heriberto was the keeper of the family history. He began each bit of information with *"Dice Heriberto,"* implying that Heriberto had said it but that it was not necessarily the absolute truth. Heriberto, who lived in Panama City, had a book about the history of the area which he never let out of his possession, so people had seen it, but few had actually read it.

"Dice Heriberto," Jaqué had been founded by Petronilo Torres, their great-grandfather, who had come from the Isla de San Miguel either to settle new ground or simply for *"aventura,"* as he put it. Jaime said it was in the Torres blood—the hunger for adventure—and pointed to Mene as an example. Jaime said he himself was the quiet one in the family, not at all like his wild brothers. He was the director of the school and the baby of twelve children in his family. He said I must have some Torres in me too, and asked if we were nervous about crossing the frontier, about going downriver to the Indian villages. I hadn't been nervous, but when locals began to ask questions that indicated concern, I began to wonder.

Adilma, Jaime's wife, asked us where we were going to sleep. "Do you know there won't be beds?" she asked?

"We have mats," Ana Maria answered. Adilma looked a little surprised. The Torres house was luxurious compared to most in the area. But it was still rustic, with a gap between the roof beams and the walls where insects of all kinds, and even bats and birds, flew during the night. But there was running water, with a bucket to scoop out water for a shower.

I have often encountered surprise from people at my desire for "roughing it," particularly, it seems, from those who live in small villages. It seems that they spend their whole lives trying to keep wilderness out—of their homes, their fields, their bodies. It is a constant struggle for survival in a place where

52

dengue fever and malaria are a reality. The concept of sleeping outdoors intentionally or choosing a more rustic life than you could afford seemed strange to many people. I thought about the impulse I had to find wilderness somewhere, perhaps because there was no true wilderness left in my country. There were national parks, for which I was thankful, but very few places, if any, where one could really get lost. I remembered a comment a friend made when I came back from Glacier Park, Montana, one year: "They have bears out there, don't they?" she asked. The pronoun said everything.

Some people around the fire were talking about a tiger that had come into the village a few weeks before. They all referred to it as *el tigre,* although it was probably a jaguar because jaguars were very common in that area. Jaime knew Victor, a man who had been attacked. Victor had come out of his house, seen a large, dark form, and thought it was a bull. He advanced and threw rocks at it. The tiger leapt towards him but apparently missed him. His dogs started barking furiously, and the animal ran off.

Adilma made a joke about the encounter and the likelihood of liquor having transformed house cats into tigers, particularly for the sake of a good story.

Everyone laughed. But Mene said he believed the account. He said he had a tiger story too, from when he was a young man.

"I had gone to this spot down the beach with my guitar and didn't know that my father had dug a trap to catch a tiger that had been roaming the premises. I stumbled into the trap, and upon falling, realized I was not alone. The tiger had fallen in also and was not very pleased about it." Mene paused to take a drink. Everyone remained transfixed, waiting for the story to continue.

"I looked the creature in the eyes, which gleamed like fire in the night, and didn't move for a full minute. The tiger growled. I realized I still had the guitar grasped in my hand. I plucked a string, and the tiger seemed to calm down. I plucked another and the tiger seemed even calmer. I tried a song. The tiger settled down on its front paws. When I finished the song, the tiger rose again, so I quickly began another. Whenever I finished a song and paused, the tiger growled again. So I played on. I broke a string. I kept playing. I broke another string and kept playing. I played all night that way, breaking string after string. As the dawn broke, I was playing with one string—the last—and it finally broke. The tiger growled and growled again, and I began praying out loud, promising to change my strings more faithfully in the future, if there would be a future." Mene paused again, took another drink, looked around the silent group, and finished his story:

"Just at that moment, I heard a shot, and the tiger fell down dead before me. It was morning, and *mi padre* had come to check the trap just in time."

I sat staring for a minute. He had kept such a straight face. I had been listening intently, as I had to do to get the whole story in Spanish, and he had told the story with such intensity, probably in response to the serious look on my face.

"Verdad?" I asked after a moment. Everyone suddenly broke out laughing. Mene was a known trickster in town, and everyone enjoyed watching a new victim fall prey.

I told him he could burn that story, also, now that he was done with it. But after a moment, I had to admit it was masterful, and found myself laughing too.

"My tiger was made up," Mene said, "but if you're going into Chocó—far from any village—you're likely to see one."

"In fact," he continued, "you're likely to see a *tigre mojano*." Everyone around the fire suddenly got quiet at his use of the words.

"Don't tell her that, Mene," Adilma chastised.

Of course, then I had to know. "What is a *tigre mojano?*"

Mene looked around the circle, and then said, "Well, given my last story, you're not going to believe a word I say, but it's the tiger that is also human, the one that has the soul of the Indian witch."

He said he had learned of the tiger from his grandmother. "The shaman is in the body of the tiger and will protect the forest at all cost. That is how you know it is a *tigre mojano:*

it will attack humans without direct provocation. And if you look closely, it has the testicles of a man."

Adilma smacked him on the leg for that one, saying, "Who do you think we are, sailors in a bar?" Then she turned to me and added to the story. She said she had heard of an herb the Putumayo Indians take to turn into tigers: it is *yagé*, also called *tigre huasca*. For protection, they wear a tooth from a tiger that came into the village and was captured and killed. They believe it connects them with the forest.

Mene smiled at Adilma's sudden involvement in the story and continued, "The shamans turn into tigers when they want to be alone. When they are tigers, they think like tigers. They are shamans and they heal, but they can also kill. The shaman teacher might even kill the student. It might be accidental, or it might be a part of the plan we don't understand. One thing is never to trust anything too completely. Or trust completely. You have to choose your way." He laughed as if confusing himself. "Anyway, my dear, all we are urging is that you be careful out there. They might not know you as a good spirit. You are a good spirit, aren't you?"

I remained quiet, thinking for too long, perhaps, and the group broke out laughing. "Stop it Mene, you're scaring her," someone said.

I let them change the subject, and we left off, as Wallace Stevens might say, "catching tigers in red weather."

13

On our last day in Jaqué, we met Luz, a young Colombian woman from Bogotá who was vacationing on the coast. She and I met in the airport bathroom when we went to check on return tickets. She had a large bag of toiletries with her. In another setting, this might have been a rather mundane detail, but I found myself eyeing her bag, secretly pleased to see a woman with more stuff than I was carrying. I had become accustomed to the economies of Ana Maria, who was unlike anyone I had ever known. She carried a huge bag of microscopes and books, but hardly a single personal item besides an extra dress. She did not even bring a toothbrush. (She did, however, acquire one later).

I've always thought of myself as a very light traveler, but in comparison, even my shampoo and conditioner felt like luxury items. At times I felt like the *niña plástica* (a phrase I'd heard in a song some children were singing) from a world of such necessities—an American. So when we met Luz, with her bag of essentials twice as large as mine, complete with hair gloss, lipstick, and mascara, I felt gratified and somewhat relieved of my self-given title.

Luz would be leaving Jaqué to return to Bogotá by plane the next morning. She said she wanted to say good-bye to the sea before she left. That night, she, Ana Maria, and I left the village and went walking quite a way down the beach. Luz said she wanted to take a last swim in the ocean. I had my bathing suit on under my clothes, but Ana Maria and Luz were just going to go in the nude. It was a long way to the water—the tide was out. We ran laughing, and they stripped off their clothes, flinging them onto the sand.

The clouds let only a little moonlight through, and Luz, with her very white skin and slim body, looked like a sliver of moon. Ana Maria, with her darker skin and hair, blended into the night, her presence almost ethereal. I felt odd with my bathing suit on, so in "solidarity" with them, I took it off, but I wrapped it around my wrist to take it with me. They teased me a little about it, but I didn't want to lose it, and the night was so dark. The waves were high, the tide fierce. We went into the rolling waves, as if we were returning, and met them one after another, huge and towering above us. We let some of them crash against us. Others we dove into or slid under like dolphins. The undertow was strong, but we were all good swimmers, and the tug from the bottom of the ocean just reminded us of the monumental forces surrounding us. We played games, feeling like nymphs splashing in the great waters, in surge and foam, and finally—fish crawling up on land to become human.

We had been in the water for almost an hour. We walked up the beach, humans now, and began to look for the clothes thrown off in the moment. We looked. We searched for half an hour. They were nowhere to be found. The current had pulled us far from our original entry point. We had no idea how far we had been swept, and we could hardly see anything. We started laughing—but nervously. Far up the beach, there were some lights from what was probably a few huts, but otherwise everything was dark.

Off to the left, we suddenly heard voices in the dark, and light from a flashlight beamed close to us. Ana Maria whispered, "Give me your bathing suit, and I'll find out where we are." But with the choice of giving Ana Maria my suit and waiting, naked in a strange land, for her to return—or approaching the people myself with my obviously foreign Spanish in my bathing suit in the middle of the night, I chose the latter.

"I'll find the clothes," I said. "Crouch down and don't move from here." I put on my suit and went off in the direction of the flashlight.

The light was being held by a teenage boy who had heard voices and had come down to investigate. He was surprised to see me come out of the dark, even more surprised to hear my strange Spanish. But I confided in him the situation and told him roughly where we had left the clothes. He led me to the place, which was about a quarter of a mile further down the beach. I quickly gathered up the items, and we walked back to the other women.

I could see their dark figures waiting, huddled on the ground, and asked the boy to stop there, telling him that I would go on from there alone. I thanked him profusely. He was very polite and went off in the other direction.

"Oh bless you. You're an absolute angel," Luz said as I approached, and she grabbed the clothes with greedy fingers. Ana Maria, too, put on her clothes with a considerable urgency.

"Yes, bless you. You see, Diana, we need you, exactly as you are. You are the practical one. Who else would get naked, but bring her bathing suit wrapped around her wrist, just in case. You saved us." She laughed then, and we all began laughing hysterically at the absurdity of the situation we had gotten ourselves into.

On the way back up the beach, we passed the boy, now with friends. They had all heard the story and were very interested in seeing these strange women who had crawled up out of the ocean.

THREE

Creciente

El saber no es distinto del soñar, el soñar del hacer.
La poesía ha puesto fuego a todos los poemas.
Se acabaron las palabras, se acabaron las imágenes.
Abolida la distancia entre el nombre y la cosa
nombrar es crear, e imaginar, nacer.

Knowing is not different from dreaming,
    dreaming from doing.
Poetry has set fire to all poems.
Words have finished, images have finished.
Abolished the distance between name and
    thing,
to name is to create and to imagine, to be born.

—OCTAVIO PAZ,
"Un Poeta"

14

WE ASKED ABOUT the boat at least ten times the next morning—at the Torres house, at Rosita's. We also asked some of the children who came to find us each morning, thinking they might be the most likely to know. But everyone had a different answer. Some said it would come in the afternoon. Some said no more boats until after Christmas. The boat had actually been there when we arrived a few days before, but for whatever reason, no one had told us about it. So we kept walking down to the dock to check.

It was a new feeling, this helplessness, a reliance on the whims of the tides and a single boat and its captain. I was still used to Miami time and the way in the States you can get everything you want when you want, provided you have the money. Ana Maria really wanted to be in Colombia for Christmas, and it was already the 23rd. Her friend Ricardo was planning to meet us at the port in Punta Ardita to take us down the coast to his piece of land to stay for a week on the ocean.

In one way, it was a good thing that we missed the boat the day we arrived in Jaqué because we ended up speaking to town officials about the environmental project in Punta Ardita, Colombia, and about how we would like to start a similar program in Jaqué—to improve the water conditions, to promote crafts for sale, to clean up the beaches, and other plans. We were told that the town council allots land and that we should write a request to set up an environmental station there. We wrote it immediately and were told we would find out the response in a few weeks, on our way back. So we saw our delay in Jaqué as a blessing, but we really didn't want to miss the next boat.

To our relief, it finally arrived with the tide in the late morning, and we went to pay, reserve our places, and fill out the paperwork to leave the country. As the officials looked at our papers and heard where we were headed, they began discussing whether the tiny village of Punta Ardita was Panama or Colombia. They were in disagreement as to whether we were actually leaving the country. Jaqué and Jurado were the two border towns, but Punta Ardita and Ricardo's place sat somewhere between them.

"*Ardita es Colombia,*" said the older official.

"No, I think it's Panama." said the younger.

"Are you going anywhere else?" they asked.

"To visit an indigenous village up the river from Jurado," Ana Maria said.

"Now Jurado, that's Colombia," a third man piped in. "Terrible town. Dirty. Are you sure you want to go to Jurado?"

"Well, we're not really going to Jurado," Ana Maria answered. "Just around it."

One official pulled out a map, and the three men leaned into it, noting where *la frontera* actually was. The older one ran a thick finger down a dotted line to the ocean, hesitated, and then made his decision: "*Ardita es Colombia,*" he proclaimed.

At first, I thought it strange that they did not know where one country ended and the other one began. But then I thought about the imaginary lines that make such demarcations and the fact that Panama was part of Colombia until the turn of the century, when the canal made Panama such valuable territory to foreign interests. This tiny checkpoint suddenly felt like a huge border, a significant frontier rich with history, the edge of the other continent.

They sent our passports into the back room, and after a few moments we were called in. A middle-aged, uniformed man with slicked-back hair sat behind a desk. An oscillating fan sat on a box in the corner, nearly blowing the one decoration, a calendar, off the wall. I noticed what looked like a bullet hole in the wall under the calendar. The hole reappeared each time the fan turned.

"And why are you two going to Colombia?" the slicked-back man asked.

"To spend Christmas with a friend," said Ana Maria. I just smiled.

He had Ana Maria's passport open, admired her picture, and asked flirtatiously if she was married: *"Casada o soltera?"*

"Prometida," she lied, saying that she was engaged.

He motioned at me: "Does she speak Spanish?"

"Sí," I answered.

He smiled. *"Casada o soltera?"* he opened my passport.

"Prometida," I answered, following Ana Maria's lead.

"Too bad," he said. "But you must have crazy fiancés to send you out to the jungle alone. And at Christmas!" He shook his head gravely at the foolishness of our imaginary men. "When are you returning?"

Ana Maria explained that I would be coming back in a few weeks by myself, as she had to remain in Colombia a few weeks longer.

"Well," he said, winking at me, "if you have any problems when you return, just come and see me." He stamped my passport and, before closing it, leafed back to the first page and kissed my picture. "Just come and see me," he said again and showed us out.

The boat that would take us over the *frontera* was a tiny motorboat, almost a dinghy. The captain was a young Colombian boy who introduced himself as Archangel. I was surprised by the name, and when he walked away for a moment, Ana Maria whispered to me that his father, Momento, had named all of his sons for angels and saints. "Let's see," she said, "there's Santo, and Lazaro, and Archangel, and I forget the others right now." We were interrupted by Archangel's return. For some reason, he had seemed unsure that he could take us, but then agreed after a short discussion with some officials.

When the plane from Panama City arrived that afternoon, the children who had been our shadows suddenly disappeared, and a half hour later a party of ten or so arrived to board the boat. The mayor of Jurado, the Colombian village close to Punta Ardita, was in the party with his family and entourage and about fourteen huge bags of Panama City Christmas purchases. There was no way we would all fit in that boat.

We did. Somehow they loaded every bag into the boat and then everybody. We were tightly packed. Ana Maria sat me down next to a young man, whispering to me, "It's the mayor's son, Nigel. Talk to him." She wanted me to tell him about our plans for Punta Ardita, the plans we would be proposing as alternatives to cutting the rain forest for lumber.

The tide had come in, and it was finally high enough to leave Jaqué. The waves were huge, especially when we first headed out into the ocean. The boat climbed up each wave, reached a crest, and then slammed down into the water. My body rose completely off the seat and slammed down with it.

"We're lucky," Nigel yelled over the waves. "It's pretty calm today. It's usually much worse."

I nodded and tried to keep my lunch down. It happened about ten times before we were far enough out in the ocean to be beyond the breaking waves. It was much calmer out there as long as we kept moving, but the wind and the engine still made it hard to hear.

Nigel began asking me questions, which I answered in a rudimentary way, about where we were from, why we were headed to Colombia. I had to ask him to repeat everything three times and still only understood about half. Tired, I finally began resorting to the "*Si*" and smiling which Ana Maria had warned me about.

"You are a very beautiful woman," Nigel said.

I thanked him, becoming used to the Latin way.

"You know, I've been feeling that I'd like to settle down soon" was another sentence I caught completely.

"It's good to settle down," I agreed innocuously, or so I thought.

There were a few sentences I didn't catch in the wind, so I just smiled and nodded.

Finally, he said something and looked at me so intensely that I knew I had to get him to repeat it.

"I said," he moved close to my ear, "that I've been looking for the right woman to float by." He paused. "I'm so glad you'll be in Jurado tonight for the disco."

I instantly stopped smiling and nodding. I wondered what else I had agreed to.

It was one of several such conversations on the trip. I was speaking to Nigel in a frank, matter-of-fact way. I realized that in his culture my behavior, perhaps my very presence, might be viewed as flirtation or invitation. I quickly began undoing the web I had inadvertently woven on the ride.

I thought about the passport official's personal questions, his kissing my picture, and what my response might have been if such a thing had happened back home. But I wasn't back home. Here, I realized that just being an unescorted woman could cause a great deal of miscommunication. Over the loud engine and with salt spray in my eyes, I found myself declining, as politely as I could, both the disco and, more subtly, marriage.

15

hweteð on hwaelweg hreper unwearnum
ofer holma gelagu, for þon mē hātran sind

on to the whale's roads irresistibly
over the vast expanses of the sea

— "The Seafarer," Anglo-Saxon

We didn't head very far out to sea, instead staying close
and riding the shoreline. It was also like riding the edge of the
forest, since the tall trees extended to the water; in some places,
they seemed to have walked into the ocean. Somewhere soon,
we would be passing the border, at least the one the politics of
this century had drawn up. The trees here had ignored the
presence of man for the last few centuries. In their isolated
positions, they had been relatively safe from loggers until recently.
Their thick trunks spoke of their age. Cedars, yellow pines, wild
cashews rose in layers up what seemed to be mountainous
land. As I stared at the shore, Ana Maria shook my shoulder
and pointed up the rocks to a waterfall we could see coming
down from high above in the vertical forest. "Just wait," she
said. She gestured something to Archangel, who nodded and
turned a bit sharply as we came around a bend, maneuvering us

closer to the land. The shoreline had suddenly become towering rock formations, rising like the buttresses of a submerged cathedral.

High above, several thin palm trees grew like flowers out of the rocks. I lowered my gaze and saw the end of the long waterfall rushing down to spill into the ocean. The boat moved so close that we could feel the freshwater spray against our skin. Now this place truly felt like a border, not a man-made one but one of two waters, the place where freshwater travels long distances back down from the sky to empty into the mammoth basin of the sea.

The rocks looked like the inside of a volcano, and I thought of how they were, indeed, the product of volcanoes. Fossils in the rocks of this region showed that they were completely under the ocean twenty million years ago, when the isthmus of Panama did not yet exist. Volcanoes had then erupted under the sea and created a chain of islands. By four million years ago, they had formed a land bridge which dramatically connected the continents, divided the oceans, and created the Caribbean Sea. Marine species were stranded on either side of the bridge, evolving into cousins that would be separated for the next few million years.

Half a world away, climatic shifts took place as a result of the bridge that had risen from the ocean. The direction of the Gulf Stream was changed, as it could no longer flow through to the Pacific. It began to flow towards Europe and Africa and warmed up the continents. Many scientists believe that this seemingly insignificant volcanic land had a hand in the development of the first humans. As the climate in Africa became dryer and the trees retreated, the first humans stood upright in order to see across the savannah. The land bridge we now call Panama did more than connect two continents when it rose. Now, millions of years later, I drew my own connections as I envisioned the events at one end of the earth reverberating and rolling through the oceans to transform the other side.

Ana Maria shook me from my thoughts and sat me down. I hadn't even realized I was standing. The boat had been moving slowly through the rocks but now gathered speed again and headed toward Colombia. "It's not far now," Nigel said, bringing me back further to this century. "About half an hour. Up ahead is the whale's tail. I always know how close we are when I see her." He was pointing to a rock which jutted out of the ocean like an island and did, indeed, look like a whale flipping her tail on the surface. If he hadn't pointed it out as a rock, I might have momentarily thought it was a real whale's tail.

"And there she is resurfacing," he said. He pointed to another rock a hundred yards away, slightly oval and on a diagonal tilt, which looked like the head of a whale emerging from the ocean. To give us a closer look, Archangel made a long figure eight around the head and the tail. The rocks were so realistic that it felt like a trick of time, as if we were experiencing the same whale diving and resurfacing at the same moment. The head was covered with tiny crustaceans which formed a white pattern. It reminded me of the markings that right whales wear on their faces like ancient hieroglyphs. No two patterns are the same.

I mentioned the right whale to Ana Maria, who said, "The markings do look like hieroglyphs. You know how they got their name, "right whales," don't you? They were hunted close to extinction because they had more blubber to use for oil and they didn't sink when they were killed. So they were the 'right' whales to hunt. They were hunted all along their migratory routes from one end of the ocean to the other. It is an ancient road they still follow, posing more dangers every year."

"You do see whales out here," Nigel broke in. "We might even see one today." As we passed the rock tail, which from another close angle looked like a mermaid draped on the rock, I peered into the dark water expecting to see anything, to have the surface of the ocean suddenly opened by the body of a huge creature that could swallow the boat in one—if it so desired.

"A whale washed up near Punta Ardita a few years ago," Nigel said. "Many of her bones are still there, and the skull—it was too heavy to move. Maybe you'll have a chance to get down there." As he spoke, the boat was suddenly greeted by three of the smallest of whales, three dolphins, which took me by great surprise but seemed to the other travelers almost a common occurrence.

"They often bring us in," someone said. "But I still feel like its lucky when they do. They like to surf the wake of the boat."

They were indeed surfing. And they were close enough to touch. As I watched the dolphins, I trailed my hand in the water to feel the speed at which they were moving. The one nearest saw my movement and moved her head to look at me, unafraid, remaining in the wake.

The dolphins stayed with us until the small village of Punta Ardita came into sight and the boat slowed down. The dolphins suddenly turned and dove into the water, disappearing beneath the surface. The boat headed toward shore, aided by the waves. I turned my head back and looked for the dolphins. After what seemed like several minutes, they resurfaced some distance away in three bold strokes, one after another, like bursts of water taking form for just a moment longer.

16

RICARDO AND CHRISTOPHER were on shore to meet us. Ricardo was Ana Maria's childhood friend. Years ago, he had dated her older sister and was some fifteen years older than Ana Maria. He was very thin, with a tanned complexion and dark eyes that seemed too big for his face. His smile showed nearly all the teeth in his mouth. But what struck me most, possibly because I was so tired, was his extraordinarily high energy. He threw his hands all about when he spoke and made wild expressions with each gesture.

"Ana Maria," Ricardo kissed her, and then scowled dramatically. "We were getting so worried," he said, in a voice that indicated deep affection but no real worry. He had known Ana Maria for a long time and was well used to her way of leaving everything to the universe.

"We missed the boat," Ana Maria said, "but it was good."

She introduced me to Ricardo and to Christopher, who both kissed me. Christopher was fourteen, blond, blue-eyed, an American. Ana Maria had told me that he had gotten into some trouble in the states with his family and school and almost every institution. His mother had sent him to live with Ricardo, an old family friend, to get him away from the peer pressure of Miami. His blond hair and blue eyes in a town of almost entirely African and Emberá descent had inspired the nickname *el gringito* (the little American).

"We wanted to send you a message from Jaqué when we missed the boat, but . . ." she didn't finish.

Ricardo nodded. Punta Ardita had no phone line; Jurado, the next town over, had one central phone line, but the delivery of messages was highly uncertain even in town, let alone a few hours down the coast.

Christopher started speaking to me in English. "I'm so glad you're here!" he said, as if he knew me. "We can speak English! I've been hearing Spanish so much, I've almost forgotten how to speak English."

"I know how you feel," I told him.

But Ana Maria interrupted us, chastising Christopher. "Diana wants to speak only Spanish while she's here, so she learns it better," she said.

"It's too hard. All those new words. My head hurts," Christopher said.

I laughed and said my head had been hurting at the end of each day, too.

"How long have you been here?" he asked.

"A few weeks."

"Your Spanish is so good," Christopher said, shocked. "You must have spoken it before."

Actually, I had learned Spanish as a little girl and had studied it for years, but the trickster in me made me answer that I had learned it in the last few weeks. "It's easy, if you put your mind to it," I told him, and winked at Ana Maria and Ricardo, who were smiling. It was obvious to any Spanish speaker that I was teasing him, that I had much more than the rudimentary knowledge of a few words and phrases one could acquire in a week or two. But Christopher seemed impressed and had a new determination to learn the language as quickly as he could.

It was Christmas Eve. We had to leave Punta Ardita quickly

because the tide was coming in, and we still had a hike of several hours down the coast to Ricardo's land. The tides were a serious force to be reckoned with in this area. The water line changed dramatically, almost a mile, and nearly a fathom in depth in some areas. Certain places could be crossed only when the water was low. At high tide, we would have to swim around the rocks—but this was only in theory because we couldn't really swim around them, given the force with which the waves crashed in. And we were laden with all our bags anyway. So we had to make time to catch the tide.

We didn't enter the town but just passed it; a few people waved but probably understood our haste. At the edge of town, we passed a huge ship which lay half-buried in the sand. Ricardo said it had been there as long as he could remember, that the people just left it, as they couldn't really conveniently move it. It had become a sort of landmark for the town as its shape could be seen from far away.

Ana Maria had told me that Christopher would be fifteen on Christmas day. "El Niño Dios," she joked. "He's come to the forest to be born."

"Then who are we?" I laughed. "Los Tres Reyes Magos?"

"I like that," she agreed. "The three wise men. Or maybe Mary. Would you like to be Mary? We could both be." She was Ana Maria. I was Diana Maria. I liked the idea of two Marys, companions seeking shelter for the night.

Ricardo overheard us. "And who am I in this holy family? Joseph? Or maybe the donkey?" he asked, shifting the great weight he was carrying for us.

At the first crossing, which was like a river connecting the ocean to the forest, Ricardo said the water had already come up too high to cross by foot. Luckily, a man with a small boat was there, almost as if he were waiting. "I asked Eusavio to wait for us in case we were late," Ricardo explained. He waved to his friend and yelled "Eusavio, *eres ángel!*"

The boat was a thin canoe only large enough for two passengers at a time. And we had all the bags to fit in as well. They sent me first with Ricardo. I cautiously stepped into the boat, which threatened to turn over. "Crouch down," Ricardo said, and I obeyed. He stepped lightly on and took several bags from Christopher to place between us. Then he crouched down as well.

The boat rocked from side to side, and I stayed as still as possible. Eusavio stood in the boat behind me. He leaned into the pole to push us away from the bank and began to pole us across. As the boat gathered a little momentum, it appeared to steady itself somewhat. "You can stop gripping the boat so hard," Ricardo said. "You're going to leave your fingers imprinted there."

I half-laughed but still held on. The boat hit the other bank, and Ricardo leapt off, held it with his foot, and unloaded the bags. He reached out a hand to help me. As I stepped onto the sand, my foot slipped, and I sank down to my knee in the water.

"Don't worry about it," said Ricardo. "We're going to get a lot wetter than that."

Eusavio deftly swung the boat around and poled it to the other side for Ana Maria and Christopher. As they repeated the process, I asked Ricardo how far his place was.

"Not far," he said. "But we still have to hurry. There are two more crossings, and there are no boats waiting for us there. The tide's coming in fast. "One time," he pointed at the thin river, "the current was extremely strong as the tide was going out, and I dropped the pole while I was crossing. The boat just spun around and headed out to sea."

"What happened?"

"Well, I headed out to sea with it," he said. "I couldn't stop it, and no one was around. The boat just kept going and going."

"Couldn't you have jumped off?" I asked.

"Well, maybe," he said. "But it wasn't my boat, and I didn't want to lose it. And the current just took me so fast, I didn't have time to think."

"How did you get back?"

He paused. "And how do you know I did?" he asked. "Maybe I didn't. Don't you know the name of this beach? Playa de los Muertos."

At my probably wide eyes at the name, Beach of the Dead, he laughed and said, "I'm only joking. I mean, a stretch of this beach really is named Playa de los Muertos. But I got back okay. I was in that boat for two days though, trying to paddle with my hands. I was fried brown like a banana when a motorboat finally came by and rescued me. Terrible experience," he said. "Terrible. Maybe I did die, at least a little."

Finally, Ana Maria and Christopher were across, and we thanked Eusavio with kisses, wished him Merry Christmas, and continued on. I told Ana Maria Ricardo's story, and she made a face at him, saying, "Shame on you—to scare her with that story." She looked at me. "Anyway, the current keeps getting stronger, and the number of days he was out there keeps getting longer every time he tells it."

"What?" he retorted. "Two days," I told her. "Two days."

Christopher said to me, "It's true. Everybody here talks about it. They say they had given him up to the sea. And then the sea gave him back."

We reached the next crossing. The tide was already too high to go around the rocks here, so we went over them instead, half-pushing, half-dragging our unwieldy bags. I caught my foot in a gap between the rocks and twisted my ankle just a bit, but I wouldn't really feel it until later.

"Hurry, we have to hurry," Ricardo said emphatically, "or we'll never make it past the last rocks. And we don't want to have to go over those."

I didn't ask why, just quickened my pace. As we reached the last set of rocks, the water had come up too high to see any way around, but Ricardo said, "It's not yet as deep as you. You can still wade around." He set an example by hoisting one of our bags on his head like a native woman and wading into the water, which nearly reached his chest. He was not much taller than I was, so I thought I'd make it, and I followed him into the sea, balancing my bag on my shoulders. I tried not to think about what a large wave might do to us at any moment, so close to the rocks.

"*Ya estamos!*" Ricardo yelled, letting us know we had finally arrived. We rounded the last rocks just in time; the waves suddenly gained power and rose dramatically, almost as if they had been waiting for us to cross safely. As we walked out of the ocean, I felt a sense of being sealed off by the high tide from the rest of the world.

17

Going up that river was like travelling back to the earliest beginnings of the world, when vegetation rioted on the earth and the big trees were kings.

—JOSEPH CONRAD,
Heart of Darkness

THE NEW WORLD we entered was an old one, forested with trees that were hundreds, even thousands, of years old, a narrow strip of forest lying between the Andes and the Pacific Ocean. This rain forest is known as the wettest region in the world; heavy rains fall, frequently at night, which sustain the lush tropical foliage in the region. Chocó, in northwest Colombia, is a vital center of forest endemism—that is, many species have evolved here that are found nowhere else.

The forest in this region falls into two main categories: tropical rain forest and swamp forest. The former covers much of Chocó and reaches elevations of five thousand feet in the Cordillera Occidental, the mountain range of the Andes which lies closest to the Pacific Coast. The latter forest exists in flatter land, particularly near the mouth of the rivers. On the riverbanks, flooding and erosion topple the trees closest to the bank, and what appears to be impenetrable foliage presides. However, this dense tangle disappears a few hundred yards in from the rivers, where the trees become more widely dispersed.

The Cordillera Occidental, like the Central and the Oriental, was formed as tectonic plates collided and forced the earth's crust up into the sky. Every layer in the mountain rock carries the evidence of eons of history. As the mountains have risen, so have they also shed sediment and worn away. They have risen and eroded in a balance for millions of years. Heavy rainfall on the western side of the Cordillera Occidental carved canyons stretching from east to west through the mountains. These were used by ancient tribes as routes of travel for centuries, long before the Europeans arrived. Through the ages, storms have occasionally turned streams into powerful floods. The floods bring huge boulders the size of houses down to the flatlands. These fallen rocks line the coast of Chocó.

During the ice ages, the rain forests, which thrive only in humidity, became smaller and isolated. Refugia (the areas that remained forested) were like nurseries for new species, and when the climate warmed and the forests once again became linked, each continued to support its own distinct families. Each forest had become its own web of life, with the animals and plants closely linked.

Eons later the cycle continues, with the tops of tall trees forming the canopy above, and the fungi and roots down below recycling the elements of life. Thousands of species exist on a single tree, and hundreds of species of trees fill a single acre of land. Bats pollinate the trees; insects suck the nectar of the flowers and, in repayment, guard the tree against other invaders. Birds and mammals eat the fruits and carry the seeds for miles in their digestive systems or on their bodies. It is an intricate community where each organism relies on the next, and the survival of one depends on the survival of the others. Humans can observe the ways of nature and find them cruel, but there is a contract which exists between beings: each takes what it needs and leaves the rest to survive.

The forest by Ricardo's house was still untouched by the logging. Ricardo told us that the part of Chocó extending down to

Ecuador had been almost completely destroyed. "And they're logging all the time up the river," he said. "You'll see the clear-cutting along the banks on your way to the Emberá village."

But here the trees as wide as houses still stood, and Ricardo said the water came straight down from the mountain and was good to drink. It came down so fast that nothing had time to taint it. On the way over, Ricardo had promised to take us up into the forest during the week; he said he could identify some of the plants but there were other people here who knew them much better, like Salazar, who knew the forest like a relative and could teach us the properties of the plants that grew there, or like Modesta, who lived in the Emberá village upriver.

"This is a very precious place," he said, "and I am afraid for its survival. It has all gone so fast, in so few years."

Even in the early days of colonization many species were brought to near extinction, like the *pau-brasil* tree, coveted for its purple dye that became all the rage in Europe and gave Brazil its name. This early mass destruction was only a foreshadowing of what was yet to come: the industrial and agricultural revolutions which made much greater annihilation possible. Rubber plantations like Henry Ford's Fordlandia destroyed the land for monoculture crops, which replaced diverse forest with a single species. This method of agriculture depletes the soil of certain nutrients. However, unlike the temperate forests with which we are most familiar, in a rain-forest ecosystem much of the nutrient cycling takes place in the forest canopy rather than the soil.

Many of these enterprises failed in the long term anyway, because of the difficulty of growing certain species outside their specific niches. The balance that made the trees flourish in the forest did not exist in these plantations. Rubber, banana, and coffee plantations all over the New World wreaked havoc on delicate rain-forest land—and still do. In recent years population growth, the creation of open land for the grazing of cattle, and logging have been demolishing ecosystem after ecosystem.

Corporations and their endless pursuit of quarterly profits and higher share values are a cause of this, in concert with the insatiable consumer culture that the corporations must feed. First World companies move into areas with such ventures as mining operations, monoculture crops, and paper mills. The paper mills are on barges that can move on once they have consumed the forest; there is not even the pretense of sustainable forestry. The tropical timber industry acts as if trees are an inexhaustible resource.

Because nutrient cycling is an aboveground phenomenon, once the rain forest has been clear-cut, it quickly becomes a desert. The soil is not rich enough for agriculture or even to graze cattle after a few years. And almost all the meat that is produced is exported. The irony is that the presence of cattle actually means hunger for the people of South America. The people are not prepared for such life-changing operations moving into their homelands to consume so ruthlessly and efficiently. Before they realize it, their worlds have been entirely eradicated, and the corporations as quickly disappear.

Ana Maria had told me a story of a wealthy Colombian she had met who had heard of the new trend in *ecoturismo*. He did not quite know what it was but he thought it sounded good. Unfortunately, he had bought a huge tract of land which he was deforesting to graze cattle. "Well, the tourists have to have something to eat," he had said.

I thought back to the man on the plane to Jaqué who was certain we would never run out of trees, and then to the tracts of ravaged land I have witnessed in my own country. I remembered what I learned in Louisiana, where so many cypress trees were removed almost one hundred years ago that still the land has not recuperated. There, it is partially because the nutria, a rodent imported from Argentina, survives on cypress seedlings; the invasive species devours any new growth. I thought of the Pacific Northwest, where I have seen vast areas of clear-cut forest from the plane, and places like Minnesota, where a huge statue of the American folk hero, the lumberjack Paul Bunyan, stands where the trees used to blanket the land. I have driven throughout the States, recognizing the trees beside the highways as the billboard wilderness that they are. Behind them, all the trees have been systematically removed. The old saying of missing the forest for the trees takes on new meaning.

The Chocó forest looked vast, dense, and impenetrable from where we stood, as it must have looked centuries ago when the first outsiders came to this land. I understood the terror they might have felt at its sheer wildness, how they might have built against it out of a basic primitive necessity to make this jungle something familiar. And yet, centuries later, far more removed from the land than the people who settled here, I was seeking to go back. It was a blessing to come to a stand of trees that was still intact, still full of old spirits.

I felt the kind of fear one feels upon entering a sacred place—not terror but awe. Time slows down, and movements seem much more precise. The senses become keener, tuning to sounds both familiar and unfamiliar—the sound of water rushing, of birds, of wind moving through trees—the smell and taste of salt from the sea mixing with pungent air from the forest; the feel of the sun hot and the breeze cool on the skin; and the incredible landscape before me, the sea and the forest in a single eyeful, with the light of very late afternoon setting the water and trees on celestial fire.

18

THE SUN FELL lower and lower in the sky as the water grew
higher and higher, and I felt the tug of forces from every side
as we reached our place for the night. We put down our things,
and Ana Maria took my hand. "We have to go, quickly, before
the sun sets." We left the others and ran to the waterfall in minutes, breathless, watching the sun mark the rocks with patterns
of late afternoon gold. The water poured out from the fount at
the edge of the rain forest. Ana Maria looked up into the trees
growing above us and asked me if I could see the little people
hiding in the rocks, if I could hear them whispering from the
branches.

"Ricardo says they have seduced me," she said, "that I am
committed to them now, that I am in love with this place." She
looked into my eyes, "In love, you understand, like a woman
for a man."

I was reminded of childhood stories I had read, of travelers
who stumbled into the realms of the little people and lived
there, sometimes for many years, got lost in a world without

time, danced with the Elf-King, slept in the trunks of trees. And afterwards, it seemed that only a single day had passed. I could only see them for a moment—the elves—before the crack in the universe closed again. It opened for me momentarily, as it has all my life, but always only for the briefest of moments.

Ana Maria bent down, picked up a handful of wet earth, and somewhat playfully drew a line down her forehead, then touched each cheek. She took my hand and put the earth in it, then touched my forehead and my cheeks in the same way. "Take off your watch," she held out her hand for it. "Your necklace, your ring." The watch had been with me for years. The necklace had been given to me by a Navajo woman the previous summer out West. The ring was from an old love.

I was a little worried about giving her my things. The pool was deep, the bottom covered with rocks and crevices, and Ana Maria had a special gift for losing objects along the way. I had seen her lose her bathing suit, her shoes, our flashlight, anything corporeal, it seemed.

She tied everything up in her skirt and pulled me into the water up to my thighs. I tied my skirt up around my waist to keep it from getting wet. She spoke some words in a language I didn't know.

"It doesn't matter," she said when I asked. "You'll understand them anyway."

Ana Maria's speech always sounded like poetry to me. I had told her once, "You speak like a poet." She had looked at me and answered, "No, you listen like a poet."

But the words she spoke now were not in English or Spanish. Maybe it was Emberá, or Cuna, or Wounaan, but they sounded like water running over rocks, like air through trees.

She scooped up water in her hands and trickled it onto my head. I closed my eyes. She did it three times, then suddenly pushed me down under the water in all my clothes. The waterfall was a few feet away. She pulled me to it, stepped under it with me, and we let it pound on our heads until we needed air again and emerged, gasping, disoriented from the powerful flood.

We climbed out, our hair streaming wild around our faces.

The sun had gone down, and the rocks were darkening with the night. "We were just in time," I said.

"Of course," she answered. Her laugh echoed on the rocks.

I untied my skirt and looked at my wrist for the time, then remembered and asked Ana Maria for my watch. She looked in her skirt where she had tied my things, but there was nothing there. We looked for several minutes, but the pool was big, the river running fast on its path to the ocean, the hour darkening.

"I think they're gone," she said.

"Gone?" I asked.

"Gone," she answered.

19

Earth and all you behold:
tho' it appears without, it is within.

—WILLIAM BLAKE

I AWOKE ON Christmas morning before anyone else and looked around at my first daylight view of the place. Ricardo had built his house just this past year, and the floorboards were still that—boards—in many places. The house was two sturdy stories, with no walls on the second floor. I had hung my mosquito net on the side of the house closest to the waterfall, the side with the finished floor. From my sleeping bag, I could hear the ocean waves in one ear and the waterfall in the other. I had fallen asleep rocked by the sound of the two waters.

I crept quietly down the stairs and navigated the floorboards to leave the house. I walked the long way around, wanting to see the high tide, and then followed the trail of freshwater leading back up to the waterfall. I looked around a little for the lost things, but I had already resigned myself overnight to their disappearance. They had probably been washed all the way to the sea during the night. The colors were different before sunrise, subdued, covered with a mist from the early morning. As I reached the pool, I heard something run off into the forest, and

I imagined it was probably a large lizard or a small mammal of some kind.

My eyes took in the waterfall, the rocks, and the thin river connecting them to the ocean. I looked up past the fall, where a trail led up the rocks into the forest. I was surrounded by a dense wall of plants, broken only by the stream and the path to the beach alongside it, and by the trail up. Few of the plants were familiar; most I had never seen before. A huge red flower must have bloomed overnight, for I hadn't noticed it the night before. It hung directly over the pool. This was a place where forest and ocean came together, and in this small pool I was between them.

On a fallen tree which served as a small dam for the pool, I saw a flash of brilliant blue. I waded over to get a better look. A butterfly half as big as a hand was moving shakily across the log, slowly opening and closing its wings. Each time the wings opened, I was stunned by the unimaginable blue. Then the wings shut again, and the butterfly became nearly two-dimensional.

It didn't fly away as I approached, and at first I thought it might be injured. It continued to move along the log in its drunken sway. I put my finger down on the log to see if it would climb on my hand. The butterfly crawled over my finger as if it were another twig and continued down the log.

I watched its progress as the wings began opening more and more frequently. What looked like a leaf blew in my direction, and I caught it in my hand. It was a remnant of the cocoon, light brown, papery thin. The butterfly must have just emerged. Its wings were so huge in comparison to its tiny body—it must have not yet learned how to manage them. The wings might have still been filling with the fluid that would stiffen their struts and let the butterfly take flight.

The wings were forming with each small flap, getting stronger and readier. I held the empty cocoon in my palm until a gust of wind blew through the trees and took it out of my hand. The same gust lifted the butterfly's open wings, and I watched it take a first flight. It circled my head and then came back down to rest on my leg—bare, it must have looked like another log. For a moment I didn't move, watching it ready itself for another wind, slowly flexing its wings.

Each revelation of blue was more brilliant than any precious stone I had ever seen. It reminded me of the Navajo belief that butterflies were created by precious stones that were tossed into the air and flew away. Another breeze brushed my cheek, and the butterfly opened its still unwieldy wings and took off skyward, flying higher and higher in wide circles until it disappeared into the canopy of trees with a final flash of color.

Still gazing up at the trees, I went deeper into the pool, and as I finished bathing under the waterfall, I heard another sound from the forest. A huge flock of birds took off suddenly from the trees above me. I thought at the time it was a spontaneous burst of energy sending them skyward.

But when I returned to the house and told them where I had been, Ricardo acted a little worried. "You shouldn't have gone alone, so early. There's been a tiger eating the pigs from the next house down the coast. And I wouldn't be surprised if he visits that pool to drink in the early mornings."

20

Ricardo had told Christopher he could have three wishes for his birthday. So like any fourteen year old, the first had to do with food. He asked for a bowl of chocolate for dinner. At first, I thought I had misunderstood, but Ricardo indeed made a chocolate soup. Ana Maria told me that in Colombia a bowl of chocolate was sometimes served as a meal. Basically, it was hot chocolate, but made from scratch with chunks of chocolate and milk powder and sugar.

The thick chocolate left a residue in the bottom of the bowl, and there was a tradition of reading the chocolate left in the cup as the Chinese read tea leaves and the Greeks read coffee grounds. After dinner, we turned our cups over, left them for a few minutes, and Ana Maria picked them up and read what she saw.

In my cup, she pointed out a large *C* decorating the bottom. And an *H* next to it. "Who is CH?" she asked, and then stopped me from speaking. "No, don't tell me yet. It is another story, still a secret, possibly even from you. But look out for him." And then she showed me the woman on fire on the sides of the cup. "There's a fire," she said, "and a woman in the center of it."

When she saw my worried face, she leaned over and patted my arm. "But don't be worried. Remember the jack pine." (We had recently been talking about the jack pine, which opens its pod and spreads its seeds only when the forest catches on fire.)

Ana Maria turned over Christopher's cup. "And now for El Niño Dios," she said, and looked in his cup for a long time without speaking. "I see fire here too," she said, "and a ship. You will be leaving somewhere soon. But first there will be a fire." She placed the cup back down in the saucer.

We wanted her to read her own, but she held her palm over the cup, stating firmly that she never read her own anymore.

Christopher broke in then with his second wish. "Well, the fortunes must be at least partly true," he said, "since I had already decided my second wish would be a bonfire." We pretended great surprise, laughed, and all headed down to the beach, where we began gathering driftwood that had dried in the day's sun. We piled it high in a pyramid shape, and when it was a pile five or six feet high, we set it on fire, watching the flames take off quickly up the branches. We sat on logs to watch it burn.

Christopher's third wish was a bottle of rum, which Ricardo reluctantly gave him, and which he first used to pour a capful on the fire and watch it flame. Ana Maria had disagreed with Ricardo's giving him the bottle. Ricardo felt that there was no safer place for Christopher to learn the harsh effects drinking can have on the body. So we all abstained, but let Christopher have the bottle, and, with Ana Maria looking on disapprovingly, let the fire take its course.

21

THE NEXT MORNING, still out on our blankets, we woke to the sound of a boat pulling in to shore. Some men had come from Bahia Solano, a few hundred miles away on the coast, to pick up Christopher. His mother was in Cali unexpectedly, and she had sent them to bring her son.

Unfortunately, Christopher was dead to the world. We shook him a little, but it took five minutes to get him even to open his eyes. He staggered up with bloodshot eyes in a green face.

"His mother's going to kill me," Ricardo said. "If the boat drivers don't." He looked at them apologetically.

But the drivers laughed and said they picked up people from Jurado all the time. "We've never had a sober passenger," they joked. Jurado was known for an entire month of drunken partying around Christmas, and the level of drinking barely declined during the rest of the year. Ricardo said you couldn't walk down the street without tripping over people sprawled out in drunken stupor.

Groaning about the ride ahead, Christopher finally made it on the boat, and it pulled away from the shore, heading directly into the waves. The men revved the engine and Christopher half-waved, holding onto the sides of the boat. We waved for a while, and I continued watching him sympathetically until they disappeared around the rocks.

Ana Maria went up to the house to make some breakfast, and Ricardo and I stayed to clean up the embers and collect the blankets.

"I'm not sure why," he said, "but Christopher reminds me of Ana Maria when she was little. I was already a man when I knew her family. Our families were close, and I saw her grow up."

"She was crazy, that girl," Ricardo continued. "I remember when I was staying with her family in the States during a particularly violent period here, and she was studying there, and she would do something like . . . come up to me and pour a glass of water on my head. For no reason. She was crazy. And then she'd laugh and run away, and I would chase her, and I knew she was going to drive men crazy all her life." And then he added, "But that time I caught her. And I put her head under the faucet to teach her a lesson."

He paused, remembering another moment from the past. "Another time, she cut me with a piece of glass."

"Why?" I asked, surprised.

"You know, I don't even remember," he said. "I was teasing her or something, and she got mad, and she picked up this piece of glass and cut me, right on my arm." He showed me a very faint scar.

"What did you do?" I asked.

"Well, actually, I didn't have to do anything," he said. She was so horrified by what she had done. . . ." His voice slowed and his eyes seemed far away. "She took the piece of glass and cut herself too, in the same place, along her arm. I tried to stop her when I saw what she intended, but she'd already done it."

He laughed a little. "She was such a wild young girl. There we were with bloody arms, and we had to bandage each other up. Strange ritual, don't you think?"

I did think. It didn't sound like the Ana Maria I knew, but Ricardo said she had calmed down. "It was impossible to be mad at her," Ricardo said. "She was so full of life, always running from one place to the next. She is a gypsy in the truest sense. She brings nothing with her except what she will give away."

He looked off into the ocean and said, "It's funny. I have always thought of myself as a traveler or of men as the ones who take to the road. But she has the wandering blood you can't contain. And you . . ." he paused. "You must have the wandering blood to be this far from home. You must have the blood."

I liked the accusation. I had never really thought much about it, but I suppose a wandering woman was less likely than a wandering man in these parts, in any parts, for that matter. But I had always felt a wanderlust, I think, from when I was a child. I always wanted to go away from the crowds, off the designated roads. Sometimes I felt as if I were running away from the world I knew, perhaps because it unsettled me, perhaps because I felt somewhat lost in it.

I wasn't really traveling in a specific direction but just to see as much as I could. In a sense, I was gathering, taking the world in to synthesize it later in my own way. Like Ana Maria, I had been searching for a meaningful hearth in which to flame. She seemed to have found it and carried her hearth with her wherever she wandered. I remembered a line from Tolkien I hadn't thought of since I was a child: "Not all those who wander are lost." Ana Maria brought it to life for me.

22

*The White Steed . . . like that chosen star which every evening
leads on the hosts of light. The flashing cascade of his mane,
the curving comet of his tail . . . a most imperial and
arch-angelical apparition of that unfallen Western world.*

—HERMAN MELVILLE,
Moby Dick

EVERY NIGHT IN Chocó, I was the first to fall asleep. We would
be lying by the fire watching the stars come out, listening to the
bats shriek back and forth above us.

The first night out, I couldn't place the sounds, and I asked
them what the squeaks were.

"*Murcielagos,*" Ricardo said.

I didn't know the word, and neither he nor Ana Maria knew
the English translation. So Ricardo, after trying to describe bats
and actually flapping his arms, finally called them rats with wings.

Not the most welcome description. I pulled the collar of my
shirt up to cover my neck. But after the first night, the sound
became familiar, and our never-ending fight with the mosquitoes made me truly appreciate the bats and their place in the
food chain.

It seemed that as soon as Sirius came up, I went down. The
others would let me sleep, and I might wake up hours later to

the stars all in new places in the sky. Ana Maria said there was some gravitational force of the dark and the stars that must be pulling me under. Sometimes I could still hear the voices of the others talking as the dreams were already taking me by storm. I stared at the constellations each night, trying to learn more shapes than Orion and the Dippers, which we can see in the city. The stars would stare back, take hold, and pull me into them.

I've always loved the night, when we are able to look out into the universe where so many other planets spin and so many stars burn. In the light of day, we are blinded to the vast reaches of outer space that might give us a truer sense of our place within the universe.

One night I dreamed myself into Sirius, the blue star, just as it came above the horizon. I traveled back into her birth, danced with the other stars being born, swirled around and was silent in that gravitational embrace. I could hardly remember a detail of the dream, but I knew it had taken place.

I opened my eyes hours later for a brief moment. Just west of the blue star the ship had come up, the stern and keel and compass visible, and somehow I knew I was meant to take it. I boarded Argo at midnight and passed through the clashing rocks, leaving behind just a bit of skin and feathers.

I saw the sacred grove where the golden fleece hung and saw my people lift it from the tree and row back down the river to the ocean. We sailed between the sheer rock of Scylla and the whirlpool of Charybdis, where the sea roared and the wild waves touched the sky. I watched Jason and Medea kill Medea's brother and cast the pieces into the sea, all in the name of this gold they had stolen. I watched Jason forsake her and she, him, as she gifted his bride with a poisonous dress and killed the children she had by him. The seas ran red with the blood of their deeds, and they cursed each other as she left in a chariot drawn by a dragon.

I watched the Argo transform into this dragon—it gathered the stolen gold and then leapt centuries ahead, taking different forms, ship by ship, from Jason's Argo to Columbus's gold-seeking vessels, to the great oil tankers and military Pegasus,

23

SALAZAR KNEW WE were there by our footprints. He had walked on the beach for a few days, noting the prints in the sand that he couldn't identify. He recognized Ana Maria's, and he knew there was another woman with her who was probably favoring her left foot (which I was). I must admit I felt somewhat tracked and deciphered, like an animal of the forest or, more accurately, a human who doesn't think to cover her tracks.

Salazar Manual Eladio had one good eye; the other one was blued over with a cataract. He had lived in the area for twenty-seven years and now lived in a house about a half mile down the beach in the direction of Jurado with his wife, Ana Julia Castro, and daughters, Yisi and Yania. His mother was Emberá, his father of African descent, from Piña on the border with Panama. He said his father had only one arm; the other had been cut off in an electrical plant. I had encountered several people in my travels through Latin America who had been maimed by machinery, all of whom spoke about it rather matter-of-factly. It was an expected hazard of a job that actually paid a wage, and most were willing to take the risk.

Salazar had come to Ricardo's house to greet Ana Maria and, not incidentally, to find out who the strange visitor was. His visit turned out to be a great source of information for me too, as I had been very curious about the plants and wildlife of the region. Salazar said his mother was an herb woman, that she knew all the plants in the forest and had introduced him to them. He took us up into the forest that afternoon. We climbed up the rocks of the waterfall and followed the trail of water into the trees. His bare feet moved quietly over the dry leaves and twigs, which I noted particularly because of the loud crunch mine made with each step. With his machete, he cleared a path, slicing through thick vines and branches with single strokes.

He stopped at plant after plant to tell us about them or show us what was inside. There was a tree whose bark was like a cord, the *burriliquo,* and he cut a piece off for me to tie around my waist. He pointed out the plant with flowers like hats, called *sombrerito de Diablo* (little hat of the Devil). I asked him about the red flower that had bloomed over the pool the other morning, and he called it the *clavellino.* Several more were blooming along the way.

Salazar cut open a thick branch of the *donguadu* tree, a light-colored limb about as thick as an arm, and held it out for us to drink from. The water poured from within the branch into our mouths like a waterfall. It tasted like pure water with just a hint of bark, a slight earthiness.

He pointed out the *trupa* and *carbonero* trees, which looked like kinds of palm, the large *bonga* tree and the *nato,* which were plentiful in the jungle. I asked him about the cactus-like plants I had seen earlier on the rocks by the sea, and he called them the *savilla.* He said *orquiria* also grew there, just at the edge of the ocean, along with a thick bush called *matapalo.* He picked some leaves from the *mataraton* (ratbush) and *resucito* (resuscitate) for a fever one of his daughters was running. He said his wife would make a green bath for her and wash her in the herbs. He also picked a few leaves from a mango tree we passed and put them in his small bag. "You can boil the leaves for a tea," he said. "It's good for a headache or for cramps."

We went further up the trail with Salazar naming trees along the way. He pointed out the *almendro* (almond trees), with their thin grayish trunks and small leaves; a fruit tree called the *tulavieja;* and the *nance,* which he said had a fruit from which the Emberá made a drink called *chicha.* He said they traditionally made *chicha* with corn, but there were many different variations now, including the mass-produced juice-soda known as *chicha* sold in various parts of Latin America.

He cut open the *sander* (or *lechero*) a tree with a rough bark. It had a milk-like substance inside. "It's like *nispero,*" he said, "which also has milk inside. It's a hard wood—good for carving. And the *nispero* milk is used to make boots."

"Boots?" I asked, thinking he might have said boats.

"Yes, boots," he answered. I questioned him again until it became clear that he meant the sap was used to make rubber for the boots.

Salazar rubbed a bit of the sap between his fingers and said it was very rich milk, one of the valuables of the continent, one of the reasons people had come here in droves.

24

EUROPEAN SETTLERS FOUND the white river that flows inside the rubber trees and fed off it, as they did the gold and the coffee and the people. The Indians called the wild milk caucho. They had used it from ancient times to make cooking pots and to roof their houses against the rain. The invading world found it could be used for everything from shoes, to tubes, to tires under every horseless carriage.

First the Europeans and later the North Americans, through companies like the U.S. Rubber Company, poked their straws into the countries' milk and sucked it to their own shores. In 1770, Joseph Priestly discovered the use of rubber as an eraser, and by 1840, Charles Goodyear and Thomas Hancock had discovered the means of vulcanizing rubber. By 1850, wheels were covered in rubber, and by the end of the century, the demand for rubber for automobile tires had soared.

In the late nineteenth century, hundreds of thousands of rubber workers were killed by jungle disease and by conditions similar to slavery. *Guardias rurales* were posted to shoot at fugitive workers, and the pay for the labor was food and liquor known as *aguardiente,* until the rubber workers paid off their debts, which was unlikely to happen. This system of labor was similar to that of the coal mining regions of the United States, a system that has been immortalized by the traditional folk song about miners and field-workers becoming "another day older and deeper in debt" and owing their souls "to the company store."

The conditions of the jungle were recorded by Joaquin Rocha at the turn of the century. Carried into the wild on the back of another man, he wrote about the treasures of the new continent as being buried in Hell:

> The silence hangs heavy, broken only by the clanging clamor of the torrents, the growling of tigers, and the swarming of infinite vipers and venomous insects . . . the plague of vampire bats that extends until Brazil, treacherously sucking in the hours of dreams the blood of men and animals. There, also, by the side of the *Brossymum galactodendron* whose trunk when incised yields milk as delicious and nutritive as a cow's, grows the *Rhus juglande folia* whose mere shade puffs up and scars the careless wanderer. There one begins to suffer the privations and calamities of the wilderness, whose horror could figure in the Dantean pages of Purgatory and Hell.[1]

Or perhaps the hell was inside the people searching for the treasure. Rubber traders sold "debtors" to each other like slaves. The people were enslaved by the very language used to describe them. One account of a rubber agency at the time has the manager claim that it was not the peons that were sold, but "the value of their debts."[2] The reality of the situation, however, meant imprisonment and forced labor, regardless of the collector. The Indians called the slave hunters who went along the rivers looking for them, "People Eaters." Rubber men sprang up all over with one purpose in mind. José Eustavio Rivera let his debt-trapped rubber worker in *La Vorágine* speak these words:

> I have been a *cauchero* (rubber gatherer) and I will
> always be a *cauchero*. I live in the slimy mire in the
> solitude of the forests with my gang of malarial men,
> piercing the bark of trees whose blood runs white, like
> that of gods. . . . I have been and always will be a *cauch-
> ero*. And what my hand inflicts on the trees, it can also
> inflict on men.[3]

Vast areas in Latin America were deforested for the sake of rubber
plantations, many of which failed anyway as diseases and pests
became uncontrollable due to the monoculture crop. Seeds were
then smuggled to Asia for even cheaper land and labor.

In the middle of the twentieth century, Goodyear turned
back to Latin America, breeding a "one in a million" tree
which yielded enough rubber to make the venture profitable
and which was also resistant to the leaf-blight. Still, however,
the money remains in the hands of big business, with workers perhaps happy to earn a small wage but at the expense of
making them dependent on the dollar. They leave the land for
factory work or the equivalent, and in one generation or two,
traditional ways are lost, and the connection with the land is
severed. In many ways, conditions in Latin America reflect the
history of North America as well, where so much changed in a
few generations of progress. In the process, much was lost and
forgotten.

25

SALAZAR WANTED TO take us to Jurado, but Ricardo said he would rather we didn't go, that it wasn't safe, especially during the holiday season with the town filled with drunks. So we just hiked down as far as the river and stopped at the cluster of rocks known as Bocavieja (Old Mouth). Across the river lay Jurado. We couldn't see the town from the rocks. Ricardo said it was tucked a mile back behind the trees, and you had to cross a guard station to get there. He said he only went in for supplies when he had to, and he always tried to time the tides right so he wouldn't have to stay overnight.

When I asked him why, he said, "It's a dangerous place. The people in that town don't care about living—only getting what they can. Too much money came through here in the last twenty years, and it made the people crazy." He circled his finger around his temple and made a face at my interest. "Believe me, you don't want to go. Be glad you don't have enough time."

So we didn't go, just stood and looked across the river, and I imagined I could hear music in the distance.

It turned out the music was real, and it was approaching. Some men were coming up the river in a little boat and had a radio on board with the volume on high. They turned it off as they approached, and I thought it was because of us, but then I realized they were about to fish. I wasn't sure if they saw us as no sign of notice came over their faces.

I had expected to see a fishing rod appear, but instead, one man took out a canister of powder and began to sprinkle it in the fishing hole. Fish began swimming through and jumping out of the water where he had thrown the powder. I stared at the operation for a few minutes, and then the other man suddenly began scooping up fish in his net. He caught them so easily that it looked as though they were paralyzed or dead. During the next few minutes, the men scooped a pile of fish into the buckets in the boat.

"What are they using?" I asked Ana Maria.

"DDT," she answered. "They think it works like magic—brings home ten times the fish."

"Where do they get it?" I asked.

"Where do you think?" she answered.

Even before I had asked the question, I knew. DDT has been banned in the States since the sixties, but the developed world still produces and markets it in Third World countries. It is still considered by many to be the most effective means of dealing with malaria in certain regions.

DDT was first synthesized in 1874 by a German chemist, but it was not used as an insecticide until 1939. It was glorified as the new weapon in the war on insects and became so swiftly and universally used that it seemed harmless because of its familiarity. For twenty years it was sprayed all over America: on crops, in neighborhoods, on people's heads to combat lice. The pesticide companies made millions, and people innocently accepted the treatments.

In 1962, Rachel Carson's groundbreaking *Silent Spring* was published, a book that exposed the dangers of widespread pesticide use. She cited terrifying features of DDT and related chemicals, such as the way they are passed from one organism to another through all the links of the food chain. Carson's book, with example after example, revealed DDT and related pesticides to be toxic and eventually lethal. DDT inhibits an enzyme in the heart muscle; it degenerates the liver; it is stored in the human body, and its concentration increases radically as it moves up through the food chain. Ironically, while causing this extent of damage to humans, it also has the effect of creating stronger strains of insects resistant to the chemicals. The pesticides also wipe out the "good" insects that keep the "bad" ones in balance. *Silent Spring* demanded that the public and the government take a serious look at the use of pesticides in America. It was a revolutionary work, and DDT was banned in the States (though dangerous synthetic pesticides of other kinds are still being used). People had a greater sense of the limitations of science and the dangers of destroying the intricate balance which exists in nature.

Forty years have passed. And yet First World companies are still producing DDT and other such chemicals and sending them to the developing world. A common defense is that there is still no better way of fighting malaria. However, an irony is that the continued use of DDT does have an impact on industrialized countries as well: the DDT returns to us in products. It is in the meat and fruits and vegetables imported, in the flowers flown in from South America and sold on the streets. Ours is a global civilization. Everything comes back in one way or another.

Ana Maria said she and Ricardo had spoken to the people about the DDT. She said, "We distributed flyers with information and put up signs around town that said, *DDT + Fish = Death*. We drew a fish and a skull and crossbones for those who couldn't read." Some of the people had been shocked and receptive to the information, but others had ignored it, saying that they preferred not to know. "What you don't know won't hurt you" is the motto so many people live (or die) by.

The young men from Jurado finished scooping the fish from the water and turned the radio back on. They started the motor and left abruptly with their buckets full and the music blaring. In the wake left by the motorboat, dead fish continued floating to the surface.

26

In Boca Vieja, at the edge of Jurado, a whale had washed up in a storm a few years ago, although no one could say exactly when. People had taken some of the bones over the years and used them for various purposes in their houses.

"Every house along the beach has a piece of this whale," Ricardo said. He himself had taken a small piece of spine, which he used as a stool. But much of the skeleton was still standing, and Salazar said we could walk inside the skull.

As we came around the rocks of the river mouth, the bones flashed white in the sun, and shadows lay in long, dark stretches on the sand. It was over a hundred feet long, half-buried, its tail stretching to the edge of the ocean. We climbed in through one of the eyes.

Jonah was cast into the sea and swallowed by the whale, where he lived in the belly for three days and three nights before he was returned to the land. Jonah doubted his faith and the uncertain path on which he was led. Who has not been tormented by such decisions about faith and the path one takes? Who has not questioned the terrible times, which seem necessary before we can break through to new dimensions? From within whale, Jonah says, "The waters compassed me about, even to the soul: the depth closed me round about, the weeds were wrapped about my head" (Jonah 2:5). Perhaps Jonah's whale swallowed him in the same way we can be devoured by our doubts—the weeds wrap about our heads. The scripture clearly states that Jonah's whale was as much within him as it was without.

In Cherokee tradition, the whale is the symbol of the record keeper, the swimming library which contains the history of Mother Earth. And it may well be, for in a sense the whale is the voice of the ocean. Its call is the song of the tides, rocking to and fro. Perhaps it is the ocean which sets the rhythm of the songs of whales. The composition of these songs is strikingly similar to human music and poetry. There is repetition and invention, imitation and change. The songs often open with a theme which is repeated, modified, and then returns at the close. Whales pass their songs to each other and take on another's compositions. One can tell by the songs in what ocean a whale lives. They change their patterns little by little, almost imperceptibly, until after a few years, they are singing an entirely new song.

Whales may make such low-frequency sounds because low frequencies are capable of traveling great distances. Their voices are extremely powerful. The average loudness of whale sounds is 155 decibels—a sound as loud as being a yard away from a jet plane with its engine at full power. Yet whales' hearing is as keen as their voices are powerful. After all, sound loses power as it propagates, and a whale must have sensitive enough hearing to detect sounds generated hundreds or even thousands of miles away. Whales born with the capacity to hear signals just one decibel deeper could extend by 25 percent the distance at which they could hear other whales. Given that sounds of the same intensity as whale calls are known to pass through the earth, some theories suggest that whales might actually be able to hear each other through the solid rock of the earth's mantle.

Some whale species use sound in yet another way—to "see" things beyond their normal vision. They use echolocation, listening to the echoes of what lies before them. When sound is used to locate food, it is of a much higher frequency than whale songs, as high-frequency sound can detect small objects. But it is also used for navigation. Blue whales, for instance, navigate great distances using sound to detect large features such as continental slopes and islands.

Whales have existed in the world three times as long as humans. They are the most immense beings we know to have ever lived on the earth. Their home in the oceans prevented them from being threatened by humans until recent years, when the whaling industry decimated many species of whales. Some, such as the right and gray whales, have become extinct over much of their original range. The most valuable products obtained were oil and baleen, the springy substance from the upper jaw of baleen whales. Baleen became highly popular for use in corsets in the early 1600s. There are two kinds of oil from whales: sperm oil and whale oil. Both have been used for thousands of purposes. The oil of blue and fin whales was used most in the manufacture of margarine. The inedible sperm oil was used as a lubricant for machinery. The U.S. military stockpiled it for years for "strategic purposes." It is prized because it can retain chemical stability under high temperatures and pressures. Sperm oil is still used for some machinery, such as the automatic transmissions of some luxury cars.

We now have the technology to obtain all of the products we used to derive from whales from alternative sources. But the whaling industry, though greatly diminished, still survives, "harvesting" whales ostensibly for "research" purposes. Though the threat from whaling has decreased, however, new and even greater dangers have been created by the pollution of our oceans and global climate change. Whales, like humans, are mammals at the top of the food chain. Bioaccumulation causes an increase in toxic substances, such as DDT and PCBs, which are stored in the body. Recent die-offs of marine mammals, including whales, are often attributed to such toxins. The direct cause of death can be hard to ascertain, as the toxins have the effect of laying waste to the immune system and the death often occurs as a result of opportunistic infection.

Climate changes such as El Niño alter whales' food distribution significantly. Perhaps one of the reasons whales evolved to communicate over great distances is to notify others of available food sources during shortage periods. Changes in salinity can affect whales dramatically. Newborns, for instance, need high salinity to float and nurse easily. Whales have evolved requiring different temperatures during different seasons. With their immense size, they need cool waters, yet their nurseries require greater heat. They migrate great distances to fulfill these needs. The progressive warming of the earth will be yet another of humans' effects on whales.

Considering the network whales create and use to survive, our noise pollution of the oceans may be one of the greatest threats to their survival. Aside from the noise created by water traffic and oil and natural gas exploration, there is controversy regarding experiments being conducted with underwater sound to measure global warming. The warmer the water, the faster the sound arrives at its destination. The overall temperature of the earth's surface could be ascertained, which might, in turn, affect policy concerning greenhouse gases. The questions surrounding such experiments are like so many other debates regarding the environment. In an effort to repair the damage we have already done, we often create potential for new damage. The costs and benefits of such experiments must be weighed very carefully.

Whales have extraordinarily large and complex brains. There must be some reason for them. One theory is that they use them to clear messages passing through the sea, which might otherwise be confused with so many other voices. Whales can hear each other over thousands of miles. Even during mating season, fin whales, for instance, are dispersed over millions of square miles of ocean. They stay connected by sound across the vast oceans, forming societies that cover immense distances. Whales truly are the libraries of the sea. The capability to store acoustic information in order to hear a distant whale signal through much background noise requires a powerful brain. Whales use their unique brain capacities to hear each other and to compose their songs.

These huge creatures embody the mystery of the ocean. In ancient times, the ocean was the body of water, the universe, surrounding the known world. The Anglo-Saxon word for whale *(hwael)* was synonymous with the ocean. Several Old English poems refer to the ocean as the *hwaelweg* (whale way or whale road). It was a metaphor known as a *kenning,* a knowing, of how the disparate parts can be connected. Even today, with our vast scientific advances, contact with a whale fascinates us like none other, even if it be contact in an aquarium. Perhaps it is the sheer size which impresses us, or the size of the facts we read—that a child could crawl through the aorta of a blue whale. What does it mean that we can fit inside the heart or walk inside the head? We know whales to be intelligent, and in most encounters with humans, they treat us calmly and with peace, even though a flick of the tail could lay waste to our tiny bodies. Despite our many studies, they remain mysterious inhabitants of depths that are beyond our reach.

As I stood in Boca Vieja looking at the world through the whale's eye, the waves began lapping against the bones, which at high tide would be nearly covered by the sea. I walked through the rest of the whale's body while it was still possible. The whale awoke memories I never knew I had, revealed directions I never knew I might take, let me see that my story was deeply connected to every other story which had gone before me and which would follow, and told me that my presence on this beach—inside the bones of this whale—was no accident.

27

THE FOLLOWING NIGHT, I awoke to an unknown sound, tap tap tapping, like a woodpecker or a drum. It went on for several minutes in that same rhythm, until the sky opened up and water poured down, and I realized it had been the beginning of rain. It sounded different on the thatched roof. I've always loved the rain, found it a miraculous occurrence on our planet—the source of life. There cannot be many places in the universe that experience rain.

It grew harder in intensity, and then the wind blew up, moving through the house with force. I looked out into the dark but could see nothing but black. I could only hear the rain and feel the mist coming in with the wind. I stayed inside my mosquito net, its gauze the only barrier to the wind in this house with no walls.

A firefly had taken refuge from the storm under the roof, and her light went on and off throughout the house. A fairy trapped momentarily by forces beyond her control, she tried all the corners then chose to circle the center. The house, like the forest canopy, would keep her from being extinguished. In the firefly's tiny bursts of light, I kept trying to see something out-side. As if in answer to my peering, a bolt of lightning streaked through the sky, and it seemed like the thunder enveloped us all at once. I had heard it off in the distance, but then, suddenly, it was upon us, rolling over the house in waves. The lightning came in from the sea, striking all around the little house, which actually shook in the thunder.

Lightning strikes have been known to come in through windows, and here I was in this house with no walls, the tall-est thing between the edge of the forest and the ocean. I had known hurricanes in Miami, but we had warnings for those. This storm had come upon us so suddenly; with no radio, we could be in the middle of a great tempest and not even know. I felt a different kind of fear in not knowing the name or ori-gin or numbered intensity of this storm, that it could, in fact, be anything. I imagined I could hear a tidal wave gathering momentum in the ocean, wondered what it would be like to be washed away like that, to have the land become the sea again. I lay inside that fierce beauty while the storm moved over us and into the forest, and the rain drummed and filled the spaces in my heart.

28

IN THE MORNING, the waterfall poured red. Ricardo said that after particularly wild storms, the mountain sometimes flooded, and some of the earth would wash down with the waterfalls—so red that it looked like blood.

I bathed in the red water regardless, its clay consistency remaining on my skin. It left a very slight tinge of red and an earthy smell, and made my skin feel smooth. We spent that day mostly lying in the hammocks strung across the top floor of Ricardo's hut, as the wet world dried itself in the sun. Ricardo opened the top of a coconut, and we passed it around, drinking the sweet water inside, and then we cut it into pieces to share the pulp.

I took a walk near sunset down to the place Ricardo whimsically called the "bat cave." In fact, it was one bat cave of many, but this was the closest set of rocks bordering the beach by Ricardo's home. At low tide, the entrance to the cave was filled only with sand and anything the last high tide had brought to shore. I walked inside, stepping over soggy coconuts that had made a long sea journey, various tree branches, and some evidence of the developed world—a bottle, a shoe, a plastic bag.

As my eyes adjusted to the light, I peered up, not wanting to disturb them, ready to dart out of the cave again if any bats decided to make a pre-sunset flight. They hung there like thousands of tiny gargoyles, not moving, suspended until the night.

Bats mastered flight eons before man's own history began. Bats and people have some physical attributes in common, and men have often looked to the bat for the secret of flight. Bats have five distinct fingers, which have bones like human fingers, and they use their thumbs to grip things and preen themselves. Bats' wings are living tissue, and a hole in the membrane will affect the bat's aerodynamics. Over time, bats have lost up to 32 percent of the bones in their hands, as horses, for instance, have lost 63 percent of their forefoot elements. Man, on the other hand, has remained relatively "primitive" by keeping all of his ancestral hand bones. Bats belong to the order *Chiroptera* (Greek *cheiros*—hand, *ptero*—wing), which includes over eight hundred species. Of all known species of mammals, one in five is a bat; an extraordinary diversity exists among the different species, and the tropical origin of bats has something to do with their great variety.

Many bats are monogamous, and they share child rearing. Vampire bats have even been known to adopt orphans, unlike most other species of mammals. The crevices in the roofs of caves create thousands of separate small bat homes. Because of their diversity, bats' mating rituals vary; some males pick a good feeding spot to attract females; others fly from miles around to a specific area to do a little wing dance, and the females choose their favorite.

Bats are a vital part of the ecology of a region. Countless species of plants rely on bats for pollination and seed dispersal. Many plants bloom only at night, and some have developed odors and shapes especially to attract bats. Wild strains of many of the world's crop plants depend on bats, such as bananas, mangos, avocados, cashews, and balsa wood, to name a few.

The existence of the wild varieties is crucial, as they are the source of genetic material to create disease-resistant strains and rejuvenate commercial varieties.

Seeds dropped by bats can account for as much as 95 percent of forest regrowth on land that has been cleared. Bats are the main predators worldwide of night-flying insects such as mosquitoes and several crop pests. One bat can catch up to six hundred mosquitoes an hour, and colonies of bats eat billions of insects in a season.

Despite their great worth to the environment, bats have been demonized for centuries. Stories of blood-sucking vampire bats have become lore over the years, when in reality most bats are herbivorous or eat insects, and all avoid humans as much as possible. They are often feared for rabies, yet far more rabies cases are caused by dog attacks.

Bram Stoker's *Dracula* had the effect of creating a perception of these small furry mammals as blood-sucking monsters. Bats do inhabit the night, and as humans are for the most part dwellers of the daylight, over time we have come to associate creatures of the night with danger. Our ancestors had reason to be afraid of night-roaming predators—it was a question of survival. The German word for bat, *Fledermaus* (fluttermouse), is like Ricardo's description of a bat as a mouse with wings and does not really endear one to the animal. In the Middle Ages, bats were called "witches' birds," and some Greek and Roman stories explain the bat as having been punished for treachery and banished to the world of darkness. But other stories do figure the bat positively, like the Hopi tale of a bat formed from dust which saves a woman from rape. Finnish peasants believed that their souls left their bodies at night and flew about as bats, much as the Hopi believed in the traveling soul which leaves the body during dream-time to gather information.

Often feared by people, bats were shot, burned, poisoned, dynamited; these actions would occasionally lead to confused "attacks" on humans. In 1963, the largest known bat colony in the world, thirty million Mexican free-tails in Eagle Creek

Cave in Arizona, began disappearing; within six years, only thirty thousand remained, a 99.9 percent decline. The cause is not certain, but the hillside there is covered with shotgun casings. Three hundred and fifty thousand pounds of insects remain uneaten there each night.

Bats are also known to be extraordinarily sensitive to pesticides—more sensitive to DDT, for instance, than any other mammal. Accumulation of pesticide residues is one of the major causes of the decline of the bat population, which is sadly ironic considering that bats function as a natural form of pest control in the environment.

In caves, bat guano nourishes a vast web of life in a place where photosynthesis cannot occur. Insects, lizards, frogs, and even visiting opossums survive off the nutritious layer on the floor of the cave. In many places the guano has been mined, mostly for fertilizer. At Carlsbad Caverns in New Mexico, the dung from *Tadarida brasiliensis* was about fifteen meters deep, and a hundred thousand tons of it were removed in the first half of the twentieth century. Although guano is mostly used for fertilizer, other uses have been found for it as well. During the American Civil War, guano was taken from caves in Texas, and nitrates were extracted to make gunpowder.

Bats themselves were used in warfare during World War II. Project X-Ray was conceived by the U.S. military to equip thousands of bats with small incendiary bombs. They would be released in enemy territory and would fly into factories and houses, where their small napalm bombs would set the places on fire. The project, however, was canceled in 1944 after several bats escaped with their bombs and set the headquarters on fire.

Bats see with sound, and sound is made up of vibrations in the medium through which it is passing. Echolocation differs in different species, but in general, they produce an ultrasonic sound which is very faintly audible to humans, like the ticking of a wristwatch. Bats can ascertain the distance of objects by the high or low frequency of the wavelength. They can detect objects as small as a wire or a flying insect from several yards away.

The distinct sound we had been hearing each night, then, was very likely the simultaneous clicks of thousands of bats on their night flight, feeding on tons of mosquitoes and other insects and saving us from being eaten alive. I looked at the bats with a new respect and quietly backed out of their cave.

29

AT THE ENTRANCE to the cave, I sat on a small rock and watched some tiny sea creatures hard at work. A few crabs furiously dug holes, darting into them and coming out again with mounds of sand. In a few hours, all of this would be covered with water. The sides of the cave were blanketed with small creatures that relied on the daily tide and the bounty it brought forth from the sea.

The tides in this area were incredible, with a variation of half a mile. When the water came up to the cave faithfully every six hours, the whole world changed. Ricardo's beach seemed to break from the rest of the world like an island. And then, as the cycle continued, the land slowly returned. These creatures knew the sea would be coming soon—they acted out of instinct or faith. Some had endured the heat of the sun all day, hiding in crevices in the mossy rocks but knowing the tide would come back.

It was an ancient environment with life that had existed long before humans entered the scene. Fossils show that many of today's ocean species existed six hundred million years ago. I was much more familiar with the biology of the Atlantic

Coast, but these creatures greatly resembled the ones I knew, though their exact classification was different. I spotted at least three types of crabs, probably a purple shore crab and a rock crab, and one known as the sand crab, more of a water dweller than the other two. The sand crabs had long slender eye stalks and plumelike antennae. I had seen them at low and high tide and while swimming. They moved about in the shifting wave-washed sand, burrowing into the ground when the waves receded. They always moved backwards: swimming, burrowing, crawling. They would lie just beneath the surface, breathing water through their gill chambers. They seemed so perfectly designed for the environment, with antennules as respiratory tubes, legs as trenching tools. They used their antennae as strainers to catch tiny organisms for food.

The very rocks were alive with animals at low tide; sponges were attached to rocks, shells, even the backs of crabs. Mythological hydroids and medusae waited out the tide, looking like seaweed growth on rocks and shells. It is small wonder they were called plant-animals by early zoologists, given their flower-like appearances.

In the small pools formed by rocks, the tiniest of fish were swimming. They reminded me of the *viuda* which we had been served in Jaqué. The word meant widow, and the fish were as thin and long as toothpicks. Once a month, by the moon, they were caught and according to superstition could not be sold; they had to be prepared as a gift. Ana Maria and I had been honored with a meal of them; each bite held about twelve tiny fish, and I had felt like Gulliver in Lilliput.

I followed the trail of a limpet in the sand. The limpet looked like a tiny volcano, with an ashy-pink shell and purplish rays, and a yellow foot set off by the light of the setting sun. The hole in the top made me imagine that a small eruption might suddenly take place. I later found its scientific name, *Fissurella volcano,* and thought it quite aptly christened.

Attached to clumps of seaweed were a few scallop shells. When they are young, they are free-swimming and move through the water clapping their two valves together, but when they grow older, they often attach themselves to a fixed object. Around the edge of the mantle were tiny eyes which shone very brightly. A sea pansy glimmered close by, with its heart-shaped disk and blue phosphorescent light.

At night here, we had seen what Ana Maria called "fireflies of the sea," which were actually dinoflagellates. If they were disturbed by a foot passing over the sand, sudden flashes occurred, and then all was dark. They glowed only momentarily. I knew these beautiful glowing beings as the blooms responsible for red tides, which can occur when the ecosystem is thrown out of balance. They thrive on very strong sunlight, and with extra vitamin B12 or some other change in the chemical composition of the water, they can overreproduce, form a film over the surface of the ocean, and cause mass death in the ecosystem below.

Thousands of purplish barnacles covered the rocks, barnacles known as "horizon markers." Able to withstand the crashing surf, they are almost always found when there is a stretch of rocky cliff exposed to the Pacific. I looked for a starfish, but none had come in. We had seen one the other day, and Ana Maria had said they were not nearly as common here. One had been washed far up by the tide, and as the day promised to be a hot one, she said it probably wouldn't make it without our help. I can still see her hike up her skirt and walk into the water up to her knees to throw the star as far as she could out to sea.

It was then that she had pointed out the tiny sea snails which left such beautiful patterns on the shore. *Caracolas,* she called them. She had shown me them before in Panama City in the bank we had visited, which had a massive chandelier built entirely from the shells. She had commented that a million deaths went into its making. I hadn't really felt a sense of loss when she said it then, but now, following the trails of the tiny shells moving about the sand, I was struck by their beauty. The swirls on their shells had been formed over their lifetimes. The shells had thickened in places to preserve the snails from attack by other organisms. The circles were not continuous but interrupted by rest periods that left their marks on the shells, like lines of growth, like the rings inside trees. The tiny creatures waited on the rocks and the shore, knowing the tide would return to reclaim them.

They knew it in their bodies, in their shells. They carried the evidence of their lives in the art on their backs. The *caracolas,* which drew such beautiful patterns on the sand, had no sense of their art—it was simply something they did. They traveled in the sand, waiting for the sea, and left as trails their beautiful swirls and hieroglyphs that washed away with each new tide. And every day the fingerprints, the watermarks of this art were new yet contained in their circles the same journey, the same story.

30

THE NEXT DAY we went to Punta Ardita to get supplies and to visit. We also wanted to look at the piece of land Ricardo and Ana Maria had bought with a grant in order to set up a nature preserve. Ricardo's friend Eusavio, the boatman who had rescued us on Christmas Eve, lived on the way to Punta Ardita, and Ricardo said he was a good guide to take us up the rocks into the forest.

We left early, as soon as the tide was low enough to pass the rocks, in order to have all day for our trip. When we arrived at Eusavio's house, he was out finishing morning chores, but his family greeted us, acting as if they knew we were coming. Germán Ivargüen and Esmeralda lived in a second hut with Esmeralda's fourteen-year-old son, Alberto Frai. They offered us coffee, which was ready, and we took cups of the strong brew. Esmeralda had mischievous eyes which shone out of her dark face. She was tall—taller than the men around her—and had an air of being in charge. She wore a colored rag around her head like a turban.

Germán and Alberto were almost completely quiet, just nodding in greeting. But Esmeralda immediately began asking me direct questions. Like so many people I had met on the trip, she asked how old I was and seemed shocked that I was close to thirty, unmarried, and had no children. By the age of thirty, some of the locals were already grandmothers.

"No husband? Never?" Esmeralda asked.

"Well, no, not yet, at least," I answered.

"What, there aren't enough men up there?" she pointed north.

I laughed. "Maybe not."

"And you have no children?"

"Not that I know of," I laughed again.

When asked personal questions, however, I tried to make sure to ask the same ones back. It's a habit of mine, to keep the balance, and sometimes it makes for good anthropology. In sorting out the relationships of the people present, I asked Esmeralda if she andGermán were married. She paused, looked at her son, Alberto, and then answered, *"parecido,"* meaning "like married."

I smiled and nodded, looking around the tiny wooden house built on stilts. Their pigs and dogs wandered underneath, occasionally bumping into the stilts and making the house shake. Esmeralda had a postcard-sized picture of Las Tres Potencias on the wall. When I pointed it out, she seemed surprised that I would notice it. She said her sister had brought it for her from Cali. On the left was a black man with a turban, in the center was a white woman with a crown upon her head, and on the right was an Indian. I had come across Las Tres Potencias in reading about Colombia and had seen the postcards with such icons in marketplaces with the *brujeria* (witchcraft). They were sold along with effigies and herbs, and some stalls even had fetuses of llamas above them, to be selected and wrapped in silver paper for spells.

Esmeralda said, "The black man is the wandering conjurer. In the center is the queen. On the right is the Indian sorcerer. They each have a power to heal. They each have a power to destroy."

This particular image of the three potencies represented three races. I have seen other depictions in which all three appear to be Indians. I have heard different names from various sources given to each potency: El Negro Felipe, María Lionsa, and Guaicaipuo—or the wanderer Huefia, Teresa Yataque, and Francisco Chasoy, from Putumayo. Esmeralda just called them the queen and the sorcerer.

Ana Maria had told me that Esmeralda was often consulted for her knowledge of the plants in the forest and for telling people's fortunes. Esmeralda asked me where I was going to be for the new year. I thought she meant for the whole year, but what she really wanted to know was where I would be when the year turned. She said she would tell my fortune then, when it was very clear. But I said we would probably be up the river by that point. I asked her how the people here would tell fortunes, and she said, "Well, they do all kinds of things. Some of them, if they want to travel, they fill their bags and run around in a circle at midnight. Others build little altars with what they want for the new year: a house, a horse, a husband. The last is the easiest to get," she laughed.

Then she looked at me and said, "You—I think you need a husband." That again. It seemed "unclaimed" women were an oddity, perhaps even a threat. I was reminded of Cochabamba, Bolivia, where I had gone for the Festival of the Virgen de Urkupina, where people came once a year from all over the country to crack off pieces of the mountain and build altars with effigies of whatever they wished for. One could buy little cars, houses, toy money, even small effigies of future husbands to place on the altar. They had given me a small set of dolls, a man and woman made of yarn and sewn together, and had said I should ask for a husband when I cracked off my piece of the mountain.

I changed the subject as usual, having had good practice with my own mother. "In Miami on New Year's," I said, "the Cubans have a tradition of eating twelve grapes at midnight."

"Well, we would eat twelve too," she said, "but we don't have grapes. So we might drink twelve *aguardientes* instead," she laughed.

"But what I do for people," she said, "is read their eggs. We have a tradition of breaking an egg in a glass of water at midnight, and at noon the next day we read the future. So it's too bad you won't be here for New Year's," she said, "or I could tell you everything."

The way she said it, I was glad I wouldn't be, so solemn was her proposition.

31

WHEN EUSAVIO ARRIVED, we left the house with him, as well as with Germán, Esmeralda, Alberto, and two dogs to hike the rest of the way to Punta Ardita. It was low tide, the wide beach unmarked by any footprints. We had to cross the river to get to the village, but you could wade across it at low tide if you knew the right spot.

I followed them across holding my pack above my head. The water reached mid-thigh. A couple of steps over, though, it was about a foot deeper, so I stayed directly behind the navigators. We hiked the rest of the short distance to Ardita, which we recognized by the half-buried ship jutting out of the sand. It was a town on the edge of the forest, the houses built in-between coconut palms, mango, and other trees. We passed the largest mango tree I have ever seen, with an incredible canopy of branches stretching high and wide. I tilted my head back to move my eyes up the trunk, and at that moment I saw her, just as Esmeralda was pointing her out.

There was the shape of a woman in the trunk of the old tree that had been there as long as anyone could remember. Her breasts and belly pushed out the bark of the trunk, and halfway up, we could see her face as if in shadows, looking down. She looked as though she had been sculpted from inside the tree, by the waters rising and flowing through her trunk, by the chance effects of storms, droughts, and other changes. I reached up, laid my hand on the tree and felt the roughness of the bark. I imagined the life rushing through her like blood, the pull of the moon on the rivers running inside her. They were like the tides, the sap that rises with the growing moon and goes down when the moon wanes.

Esmeralda opened a small pouch around her neck and showed me a seed. "This was from a twin," she said. "I planted one behind my house. The other I wear around my neck. As I watch the tree grow, I know how great a tree there is inside this very seed."

Olga Gonzalo had seen us by the mango tree and came out to meet us. She was about thirteen with flashing eyes and light-brown skin. She smiled when she saw my hand against the trunk. "I see you've met the woman tree," she said. Olga was one of twelve children—including a set of triplets—of Ana Julia and Dagoberto Gonzalo. Their family had moved from Jurado to make their own colony out on the point a few generations ago, and the town consisted mostly of their family. Some Emberá lived in the town, and a few nonrelated Colombians. Ricardo had said they allowed other people to live there so that the community could be recognized by the government as a town.

Olga took us to meet her mother, Ana Julia, and her grand-mother, who, upon taking my hand, said her name slowly and distinctly: Angela Rosa Garcia, with a particular emphasis on the last name. Angela Garcia had come to the town with her daughter, who had married a local, and she stated her different last name as if it distinguished her from all the Gonzalos in town.

Ana Julia had a little store in town about the size of a closet, and she cooked meals for people passing through or stopping for supplies. She knew Ricardo well and had put on a pot to boil when she spotted us coming up the coast.

We told her we were headed up into the forest to see the land acquired for the nature preserve. "That's way up there," she said. "You must eat first, or you'll never make it."

We laughed and told her we had just had breakfast and coffee and that we would come by in the afternoon after seeing the land.

"Well, go ahead then, but mark my word, you'll wish you had a little more something in your bellies for a hike like that. Mark my word." She said it almost as if putting a spell on the journey.

But we thanked her and moved on through town, where thirty or so children with very similar faces stopped playing to stare at our odd little group headed for the mountain. At the edge of town, the land immediately became steep, and Germán cut us walking sticks with his machete. The path was relatively clear as if it had been traveled recently, but Eusavio and Germán went first with their machetes to clear the way for us as much as possible.

The forest was dense and lush, many degrees cooler than the beach, and filled with the sounds of birds. I spotted a beautiful one with a black-and-yellow tail which Esmeralda told me was a *mochilero*. It made a long, warbling cry which sounded like the music of an unknown flute. Esmeralda pointed out a palm tree that had what looked like small sacks of straw dangling from its leaves. We watched a black-and-yellow bird fly up into the nest. The nests were as long as an arm, tubular, with a wide bottom, and looked as sturdy as a woven basket. They swayed with the wind and made me think of cradles rocking in the trees.

I could imagine the baby birds in their eggs learning the rhythms of the wind long before they cracked through their shells and opened their wings. In the cradle of our mother's bodies, we learn our first poems. We feel the rhythm of her movement like the swaying of trees in the wind.

In the hammock at Ricardo's, I could fall asleep so easily to the tune of birds and crickets and many sounds I could not name. A different rhythm enters our bodies when we leave the fast-paced world of streets and machines, when we sleep by the dark of night and wake by the light of sunrise.

We hiked for several hours up through the forest. We had not brought any water with us, and just as my dry mouth began chastising me, we heard the sound of a waterfall pouring down on the rocks. We stopped at the opportune fountain. The men took off their hats and used them as cups. With a few deft folds, Esmeralda quickly fashioned a little drinking scoop from some palm leaves, filled it with water and handed it to me to drink. The water was deliciously cool, and before I finished drinking she had made two more cups and given one to Ana Maria. "Keep them for later. They work better than hats," she said.

Eusavio looked at my tired face and promised me we were almost there. I wasn't all that tired, but I was feeling quite hungry by that point, to tell the truth, and Ana Julia's offered meal kept appearing in my thoughts.

Luckily, the others were just about as ready for food, and even more luckily, we had our pick of wild fruit trees just ahead. Esmeralda sent her son, Alberto, to climb the *mandarina de China* to get us some Chinese mandarins, a juicy citrus which we drank down. She also picked some guava from the trees growing just ahead. I had eaten guava many times back home in pastries, but I had never bitten into a fresh guava fruit on a hungry stomach. The fruit was firm, the taste tangy but sweet, and it seemed like a gift sent by the gods.

As we walked the rest of the way up, we also found a fruit they called *guama* that had a hard, textured outer shell. A white furry edible part covered each of the seeds, and we ate the fruits one after another, spitting the seeds back into the forest. "When you harvest, you have to plant," Esmeralda said, and spat another seed.

"Actually, it's one of our purposes on this earth—to scatter seeds," Ana Maria added, smiling. "And with our long hair, we're definite assets to the forest." I laughed, well used to picking seeds from my clothes and hair, secret travelers determined to journey great distances.

Somewhat refreshed by our small harvest, we found the path up to the edge of the land, where the rocks jutted out over the ocean, hundreds of feet up. I could smell the ocean spray even that far from it and could feel the power of the waves as they crashed against the rocks again and again. The earth seemed to shake each time, but it was probably just the roar and the echo of the waves in my ears. I felt the mutable nature of the land underneath me, poised over the water for only a few more centuries before the vast sculpting power of the ocean might change this geography under my feet. All along the coast lay huge rocks, as big as buildings, which had been sculpted by the force of water—the force of the freshwater pouring down from the forest and the power of the ocean swirling and pounding the rocks into new forms.

And each rock that lay in its new home separate from the mountains acquired new characteristics as centuries passed. Many of the rocks had long ago been given names, some of which had changed according to perspective. But others had remained over generations because their faces were so distinct, because the mermaid was a mermaid and the whale was clearly a whale.

I sat on this point of land above the Pacific and looked down the coast of forest extending almost into the ocean and could feel the ancient union between these forces—the rich life supported by freshwater flowing down into the sea. The history of the planet lay in the mountains behind, the salty sea extending out, and the rivers of freshwater running down to join the two, moving mountains as they flowed their course.

Some droplets of water remained in the cup of leaves Esmeralda had given me. I put a drop on my tongue. Water—it is a substance in such perfect balance. Any hotter and it would evaporate. Any cooler and it would freeze. It gives us life and forms 90 percent of our bodies. Where there is liquid water, there is life.

There might be other life in the universe—there probably is. But the forces on this planet that came together to create the DNA which would subsequently build every living thing were truly miraculous. I could feel the planet's origins around me, from the deep hot center to the crystallized rocks and mountains to the cool atmosphere and blue sky which the plants had slowly sighed into existence. It was the Earth, alive with changes herself, which created us and everything we know—out of fire and air, earth and water.

32

It was almost sunset when we returned to Punta Ardita, and we decided to stay a few hours to rest and wait for the tide to subside before attempting to return home. Ana Julia laughed when she saw our exhausted faces. None of the locals did that hike except for a specific purpose. The idea of going all the way up just to have a look around seemed crazy to her.

But she had dinner ready and served us big bowls of snapper soup with yuca and carrots and potatoes, and we ate like the hungry travelers we were. Another of Ana Julia's children, Azael, ate dinner with us; he had come from Jurado on the boat that afternoon to see his son, whom he had named John Lennon. Azael worked with loggers in Jurado, since there was money to be made, but his family stayed in Punta Ardita. He had a Walkman around his neck and a big, flashy watch on his wrist.

John Lennon wandered around people's legs with not a stitch of clothing on. Around his neck, however, was a large bead. I had noticed that all the babies wore such jewelry around their necks. Azael told me they were for *mal de ojo* (bad eye), which I first thought meant some biological illness such as conjunctivitis but then understood that it referred to the evil eye. Azael said the evil look was too common to let babies go about unprotected. "When you are older you can fight it off," he said, "but as a baby you are defenseless." He said he had known unprotected babies to fall ill with a terrible stomach illness as a result of *mal de ojo*.

Esmeralda added that the look could sometimes even be unintentional. It took on a power of its own. She called it *envidia* (envy) that leaps from the eyes like a beast to devour what it sees. She opened the pouch around her neck and took out a branch of dried rosemary and broke off a piece in my hand. "You can burn this as an incense to protect your house from *envidia*," she said, and then added. "Emotions can be powerful magic. They can transform things."

Esmeralda continued with a story about envy between two women—how the one, in her envy of the other, transformed her in her own mind into something less than she was. "In that way, anyone can be a *bruja* (witch)," she said. "The power is there. This woman cut the woman she envied with words that could be taken two ways. And the woman hardly noticed she was being cut, until one day she felt transformed into the very ugliness the other woman felt for her. The words were very powerful. Like spells."

The word *envidia*/envy has origins prior to the Middle Ages. In 1369, Chaucer spoke of the earth envying the heaven: "As thogh the erthe envye wolde, To be gayer than the heuen." The word derives from the Latin, "invehi": passive form of "invehere," to attack, contend for mastery. The old word had the connotations of both invitation and challenge. But it is often a challenge from the secret recesses of the mind, known only to the one who feels it. Coleridge referred to the emotion as being "envy-mad." Joseph Campbell called it a dragon burning from the secret cave inside us. The emotion is hot like the fire from a dragon's mouth; it keeps us in darkness and in chains we hardly recognize.

Envy has powerful energy. We have probably all felt it, both burning inside and burning outside from someone else's gaze or words. It is present in the archetypal stories of human existence. Cain killed his brother Abel because he envied the praise his brother had received, and he was subsequently banished forever to be a restless wanderer on the earth. In *Othello*, Iago's envy of Cassio and his scheming for revenge set in motion Othello's fatal jealousy for Desdemona. Iago claims: "If the beam of our lives had not one scale of reason to poise another of sensuality, the blood and baseness of our natures would conduct us to the most preposterous conclusions," yet ironically he is ruled by the sheer force of his envy. Envy is a fierce master and sets in motion chains of events we rarely anticipate. I have felt it to be one of the most palpable emotions, and the amulet seemed not such a bad idea.

But faith can be as powerful a magic as envy: what people believe will happen often happens. Esmeralda said that when she lived in Cali she had cured white women's jewelry all the time to protect them from something or to bring them love or money. They asked for aid in the business of their world, and she sometimes made up spells to satisfy them. "I make it up," she said. "But it makes them go away content. So it works. It is good medicine."

FOUR

La Violencia

*And I saw, and behold a white horse: and he that sat
on him had a bow; and a crown was given unto him:
and he went forth conquering, and to conquer.*

*And when he had opened the second seal, I heard
the second beast say, Come and see.*

*And there went out another horse that was red:
and power was given to him that sat thereon to take
peace from the earth, and that they should kill one
another: and there was given unto him a great sword.*

*And when he had opened the third seal, I heard
the third beast say, Come and see. And I beheld, and
lo a black horse; and he that sat on him had a pair of
balances in his hand.*

*And I heard a voice in the midst of the four
beasts say, A measure of wheat for a penny, and three
measures of barley for a penny; and see thou hurt not
the oil and the wine.*

*And when he had opened the fourth seal, I heard
the voice of the fourth beast say, Come and see.*

Revelation 6:2–7

33

Ricardo had gone to school in Bogotá to study biology and animal husbandry, but political unrest had made a formal education rather difficult for him. His experience was typical for anyone going to school in Colombia in the seventies—or actually in most of the last fifty years.

The years of conflict are probably a factor in Ricardo's relative isolation at this point in his life. He chose to drop out of society and live on a piece of land as far from civilization as he could get. "Still today, in every city here, in every town," Ricardo said, "there's a *matón del barrio*, the hired killer. Everyone in the neighborhood knows that he's for sale and that he does half the killings in town. But it's like anywhere. People are afraid to confront him, and anyway, he's just the weapon, really. The mind behind the murder still has to be found."

"Colombia is a land of extremes," he said to me. "It's really one of the only wild places left in the world. You can do anything you want here. You can kill someone, and the law won't have much to say about it. Or you can choose to leave it all behind and go live in the woods somewhere. Personally, I chose the latter."

In fact, until 1997 there was a law on the books in Colombia which protected anyone who killed in a combat situation for political reasons. The law, which was created during the many political upheavals of the nineteenth century, stated that "rebels and seditious peoples will not be subject to penalties for punishable deeds committed in combat, as long as they don't constitute acts of savagery, barbarity, or terrorism." As one can imagine, the law itself, as well as the last three categories, has been quite loosely interpreted. The law was finally overturned in 1997, a ruling which has elated military officers and troubled politicians and those working to establish peace with leftist guerrillas.

Ricardo's family had tried for the most part to remain neutral, although it is hard to remain neutral in a community where bullets are likely to whizz by your ear on your way to school. Ricardo said his family lived through the bloodiest days of *La Violencia,* which began in the forties, setting off violence that has lasted until the present time. It began with a struggle between the Liberal and Conservative parties, but there was a definite element of class struggle in the ensuing situation. The somewhat-feared, somewhat-scorned Liberal leader Jorge Eliécer Gaitán, known to his own party as "The Wolf" or "The Idiot," had become popular enough to threaten the political order. When he was assassinated, a storm of violence swept through the countryside. In *Open Veins of Latin America,* Eduardo Galeano sums up the horrors of La Violencia:

> First the spontaneous *"bogotazo"*—an uncontrollable human tide in the streets of the capital; then the violence spread to the countryside, where bands organized by the Conservatives had for some time been sowing terror. The bitter taste of hatred, long in the peasants' mouths, provoked an explosion; the government sent police and soldiers to cut off testicles, slash pregnant women's bellies, and throw babies in the air to catch on

bayonet points—the order of the day being "don't leave even the seed." Liberal Party sages shut themselves in their homes, never abandoning their good manners and the gentlemanly tone of their manifestos, or went into exile abroad. It was a war of incredible cruelty and it became worse as it went on, feeding the lust for vengeance. New ways of killing came into vogue: the *"corte corbata,"* for example, left the tongue hanging from the neck. Rape, arson, and plunder went on and on; people were quartered or burned alive, skinned or slowly cut in pieces; troops razed villages and plantations, and rivers ran red with blood. Bandits spared lives in exchange for tribute, in money or loads of coffee, and the repressive forces expelled and pursued innumerable families, who fled to seek refuge in the mountains. Women gave birth in the woods. The first guerrilla leaders, determined to take revenge but without clear political vision, took to destroying for destruction's sake, letting off blood and steam without purpose.

The names adopted by the protagonists of violence—Gorilla, Evil Shadow, the Condor, Redskin, the Vampire, Black Bird, Terror of the Plains—hardly suggest a revolutionary epic, yet the scent of social rebellion was in the couplets sung by their followers:

> I'm just a campesino,
> I didn't start the fight,
> But if they come asking for trouble,
> They'll get what's coming to them.[1]

Ironically, during the period of La Violencia, the amount of capital accumulation was so great that historian Alberto Lleras Camargo stated in his writings that blood and accumulation of wealth went hand in hand. And Eduardo Galeano has repeatedly posed the question as to whether the prosperity of a class was really identifiable with the well-being of a country. For the industrialists and the urban bourgeoisie, the violence meant profit:

industrial production was high, coffee prices soared because of low volume. Meanwhile, the poor were dying by the thousands in the coffee-growing regions.

The effects of La Violencia in Colombia pervaded the next few decades in the vast gaps between the financial resources of the rich and the poor. The two traditional parties, the Liberals and the Conservatives, had a virtual monopoly on political life, and earlier peasants' and workers' movements of the twenties and fifties had been mostly wiped out by violence.

In the seventies, various movements stirred again. The popular response grew with great geographic and political diversity and had banana workers demanding union recognition in the North, peasants fighting for land in the East, Indians demanding territorial and cultural rights, and black people organizing for the first time in Chocó.

In cities, urban workers fought traditional party control. Situations that had been acceptable became intolerable as hordes of people moved to the cities. Essentially, a situation of "behavioral sink" (the outcome of collecting beings together in unusually great numbers with too few resources) occurred. From the mid-sixties to the eighties, guerrilla warfare was prevalent, and violence erupted sporadically throughout the country. Most of the guerrilla factions formed with strong peasant and worker support, and much of the violence was seen as strife between the haves and have-nots.

The presence of strong guerrilla movements controlling the countryside gave rise to a booming drug industry. Initially, the guerrillas used drug profits to finance their operations. It was not long before government officials themselves became involved in the drug trade. In the early 1970s, marijuana, grown first in Urabá, became the dominant drug export of Colombia. It was exported to the United States in the banana boats, often with police and customs complicity. When the United States began to monitor boats from the Urabá region more carefully, La Guajira became the choice place of cultivation. North American drug dealers financed much of the crops. In the late seventies, President Turbay, under suspicion of involvement, yielded to U.S.

procedures to eliminate the crop. Ten thousand troops entered the area and used violent means against the peasant workers. In the process, many officers and soldiers became involved in the drug traffic themselves, and the Minister of Defense gave the task of drug suppression to the police.

The United States had been behind the drug removal campaign in Colombia, though marijuana was being grown all over the States. In 1980, 40 percent of the U.S. market was homegrown, and most of the rest came from Jamaica. The regions that had grown marijuana in Colombia experienced an increase in poverty, unemployment, and crime. Worse, marijuana was replaced with a far more lucrative and dangerous product—cocaine. The amount of cocaine increased from 15 tons in 1978 to 270 tons by 1988. The demand for cocaine in the United States became a terribly corrupting influence in Colombia. There, young people increasingly smoked *basuco* (cocaine paste mixed with marijuana or tobacco). In anger, one Colombian youth leader asked, "Wasn't it they [the United States] who turned the coca leaf into a diabolical drug for sale in classy city discotheques?"

Colombia had never been more than one of the players involved in the wholesale business of marijuana. The loss of government control over much of the countryside, the social disintegration that followed La Violencia, and the potential for unimaginable profits combined to make Colombia the world's leading exporter of cocaine. By the mid-1980s, Colombians controlled an estimated 70 to 80 percent of the world's cocaine trade. The country became the center for processing and marketing of coca from Peru and Bolivia. In 1984, Colombia's cocaine lords had an annual income of about U.S.$11 million. It is the illegal nature of the drug that explains the huge profits associated with cocaine. One kilogram of the raw material of cocaine paste may cost $800. After being purified, refined, and unloaded in a consumer country, the original kilo can be resold for $50,000.

Naturally, an extraordinarily wealthy cocaine mafia emerged in Colombia. In 1987, *Fortune* magazine presented two leading drug barons, Jorge Luis Ochoa and Pablo Escobar, as two of the twenty richest men in the world. Several times they reportedly even offered to pay off Colombia's foreign debt. They amassed their riches after becoming acquainted with the possibilities of the U.S. market. The drug mafia employed over half a million people: chauffeurs, cooks, assassins, not to mention those involved in coca production itself. The mafia eased the effects of the industrial recession in Medellín's textile industry in the early eighties. They bought huge tracts of land and set up cattle ranches and other businesses in the financial sector.

There wasn't much in Colombia for the drug barons to buy, so they got their hands into many U.S. companies. Much of the money was deposited in U.S. and European banks. Drug money did enter Colombia "officially" through the *ventanilla siniestra* (side window) that was opened in the Central Bank in the mid-seventies. It allowed the deposit of foreign currency with virtually no question about its source, in an effort to take in black-market dollars that were adversely affecting the value of the country's exports. Cocaine, however, was only one factor in financing the external trade balance. Coffee, oil, and coal earnings as well as Colombia's history of flexible economic management aided the economy in the difficult eighties.

Cocaine bosses came mostly from humble origins; 70 percent were of peasant origin and 55 percent had only primary education. Pablo Escobar himself was a child of the Medellín slums and had been a car thief. These *nouveaux riches* attempted to enter the world of the previously ruling elite. Though the old elite were not eager to open their exclusive clubs to drug barons seeking social legitimacy, they did, in fact, create political alliances with them and with the army. These alliances were directed against popular anticorruption leaders and activists, many of whom were murdered.

The major drug cartels in Colombia—the Medellín and Cali cartels—experienced their downfall in the early and mid 1990s. Members of the cartels—Pablo Escobar, Gonzalo R. Ochoa, Fabio Ochoa, and Jorge Ochoa—became legendary figures throughout Colombia. They were both loved and hated. Pablo Escobar, in particular, draws both types of response. He is hated by those affected by the terrorism but revered by those who benefited from his generosity. In Medellín, he built eight hundred free homes for Medellín's poor in a *barrio* now known as Pablo Escobar. He employed thousands of people in the gangs he set up to handle his enemies.

In the early 1990s, as authorities sought to take Escobar into custody, he indiscriminately killed hundreds of police officers and set off dozens of bombs. He even bombed a jetliner with over a hundred people aboard out of the sky in an attempt to kill two enemies. Many felt that he had launched a war not against the state but against the whole world. Escobar was finally jailed in 1991 but later escaped and was gunned down in 1993. The Medellín cartel was dissolved with the death of Escobar, and the Cali cartel saw its downfall two years later.

The drug cartels pumped money into Colombia during the last twenty-five years but also created even greater inequities than had previously existed. Through the drug trade, Colombian peasants had found a way to climb the ladder and to claim some of the world's wealth for themselves. Unfortunately, those left in the slums paid the price as they became the foot soldiers and most frequent victims of the drug violence.

34

THE PEOPLE OF African heritage are referred to as *cimarrones* in Colombia. I first heard the term as an acronym of the National Movement for Human Rights of the Black Communities of Colombia (CIMARRON). Later I found out the origin of the word. The Spanish *cimarron* was first used in Hispaniola to refer to the Spaniard's feral cattle, then to Amerindian slaves who escaped, and by about 1530 mainly to Africans who were fleeing slavery. According to linguist José Arrom, the word actually derives from an Amerindian (Arawakan/Taino) root; it is one of the first linguistic coinages in the post-Columbian Americas.

The word *cimarron* came to mean runaway or fugitive; it spawned the English words *maroon* and, interestingly, *Seminole*. The Seminoles did not exist as a tribe before the arrival of Europeans and Africans; they were a community composed of Creeks, a few other tribes, runaway slaves, and some whites who chose Indian society. The Seminoles' refusal to surrender their African-American members was the real cause for the First and Second Seminole Wars (1816–1818, 1835–1842). Whites attacked not because they wanted the Everglades, which had no value to the United States in the nineteenth century, but to destroy it as a refuge for runaway slaves.

Most of the settlements on the Pacific Coast in Colombia were formed by rebel slave populations and their descendants. Slaves were brought to Colombia mainly to work in the mines, and from the very beginning there were major revolts. Escaped slaves formed *palenques,* refuge communities in the thick tropical forests, and kept their cultures alive there. In the 1590s, authorities in Colombia officially ordered individuals harboring fugitive slaves to turn them in; they issued a lengthy and elaborate decree as to the rules and penalties. José Urueta cites this document in his 1890 *Documentos para la historia de Cartagena:*

> Furthermore, it was agreed and decided that: no slave, male or female, shall run off and leave the service of his master under penalty—should his absence be for as long as 15 days—of receiving 100 lashes as follows: he shall be tied up at the city pillory in the morning, decorated with strings of bells around his body, whipped 100 times, and left in that position all day long for the other slaves to see. And whosoever dares to remove him from the pillory during that day shall have to pay a fine of 20 pesetas, which will go to the judge, the accuser, and the Council in equal shares.
>
> Furthermore, a captured runaway who has been absent from the service of his master for more than one month shall have his genitals cut off in public and displayed at the city pillory, so that other slaves may come to realize the consequences.
>
> Furthermore, captured slaves who have been runaways for over a year shall be sentenced to death.
>
> Furthermore, female slaves who have been runaways for more than 15 days shall receive 200 lashes in the same manner as male slaves who are caught 15 or more days after having run away.

Furthermore, whoever captures and keeps a slave who has been away from his master for more than 15 days and does not return him to his rightful owner shall have to pay a fine of 5 pesetas, plus a contribution of 10 pesetas to encourage others to pursue runaways.

Also, a large enough force is to be formed to go on expeditions against the maroons, who live in the wilderness, and to bring them back to the city. Since some of these Negroes are going around and defending themselves with weapons (like those used by the authorities), the Government has decreed that individuals who foresee a threat of danger from maroons shall have permission to kill them, if and when they cannot be captured alive. Such permission has been granted especially since it would be advantageous to clean up the territory where these Negroes are based and from where they raid the neighboring roads. Therefore, those individuals who kill Negroes for these reasons shall not be subject to any form of legal prosecution.

Furthermore, settlers of neighboring areas shall be obliged to help pursue and capture maroons, whenever the commissioned authorities call upon them to do so. They shall be reminded on such occasions of the material benefits which will accrue from the elimination of maroon raids on their own property.

Furthermore, if an Indian or a Spaniard captures a runaway slave in this way, the slave's owner shall have to pay him 10 pesetas per captured slave. If either the runaway's corpse or his head (which would confirm his death) are returned to the owner, the payment shall be 5 pesetas, which shall come from the same source as above.[1]

But despite such harsh retribution, slaves fled in great numbers to the forests of Colombia. Domingo Bioho was the first to lead a slave revolt. He claimed to have been king of an African state, and with his band of thirty Negro men and women escaped to the marsh and defeated the twenty slave owners who pursued them. Domingo became known as King Benkos and founded and defended the *palenque* of San Basilio.

During one struggle, the Africans captured the Spanish Captain Francisco de Campos. As the story goes, at the *palenque* he found Bioho's daughter, Princess Orika, who had been his lover when her mother, Queen Wiwa, and her brother, Prince Sando, were slaves of Captain Alonso de Campo. Queen Wiwa and Princess Orika cared for the prisoner, but during an attempted escape he was shot, and Orika was sentenced to death.

After many battles, Governor Don Diego Fernandez de Valasco decided that the cost of fighting Bioho had already been prohibitively high. He proposed a treaty that gave the rebels certain rights. The treaty contained some strange provisions, such as that Bioho would not be permitted to use the title: "King of the Arcabuco." In such manner, San Basilio became a community recognized by the government.

During the early colonial period, there was a serious imbalance of male to female slaves. The imbalance was even greater among the *cimarrones*, because more men had made successful escapes. The men were well aware that fights over "rights in women," as they were called, could rend their communities apart. Many groups tried to solve this problem by capturing Indian women. Women were considered a form of property all over the New World, regardless of color. It was their capacity as "property" that accounts for the vast race-mixing of the New World.

The *palenqueros* in Colombia remained virtually isolated until the end of the nineteenth century. They were self-sufficient, growing rice, corn, peanut, banana, and manioc and grazing cattle. It was sugarcane agriculture that brought them into the national community. The *palenqueros* entered the sugarcane industry, received salaries, and began to break from the traditional way of life, which caused their kinsmen deep regret. As Richard Price comments, "Some even wept as one does for a funeral, particularly for those who were going off to work on the construction of the Panama Canal or on the banana plantations of the Department of Magdalena."[2]

35

SALAZAR CAME BY one afternoon to bring us some supplies from Jurado—kerosene, coffee, powdered milk, and some bananas from his trees. His twelve-year-old daughter Yisi was with him. She stayed with a family in Jurado during the week in order to attend school. We invited them in for hot chocolate.

Yisi had a history book with her. As we sat around the hut drinking chocolate, I asked her if I could see it, and she shyly passed it to me. The Spanish was easy to understand.

I've always been interested in the presentation of history, particularly for students. When I studied in East Germany during college, I acquired an East German textbook about U.S. history for students studying English. It was quite fascinating to read a socialist country's slant on the history of my country, which was presented as an evil capitalist empire.

As I leafed through Yisi's schoolbook, I stopped on a paragraph-long account of El Dorado and wondered how Salazar and Yisi, part Emberá, part black, viewed the history of gold in their country. As if reading my mind, Salazar came up behind me, leaned forward, and put his finger on one of the sentences in the book, which listed a few names of Europeans who had searched for El Dorado. "Do you know his story?" he asked, his finger under Jimenez de Quesada. "He was one of the first ones to hunt for the gold. He was the one who took an animal of gold from the Templo del Sol in Boyocá. He and all of his men died horrible deaths."

"They came to take out the gold," he continued, "That was the reason they came here in the first place, looking for the riches under the earth. But they couldn't be taken away without a price. Quesada's men and the others that followed were punished with their lives and, forever after, with their sanity. They left a curse on their descendants. They left a madness that still lives inside the people."

It sounded like the story of Lope de Aguirre, which had always brought chills to my body. In the 1500s Aguirre, in search of El Dorado and in search of political power, went mad in the jungle and denounced the king of Spain. He and his men chose one among them and crowned their own new monarch of the New World: Fernando. They had searched and searched for the legendary golden lake but found only hunger, fever, and death. Aguirre went mad with the desire for conquest of every province and killed the very king he crowned. He killed the captain of the guard and the lieutenant-general and four captains. He appointed new ones and killed them as well. He killed everyone he imagined plotting against him and, abandoned by his men, he murdered his own daughter to "protect" her from revenge. He was finally killed by his own troops; his body was quartered, and pieces of it were displayed in marketplaces throughout the colony.

I mentioned Lope de Aguirre to Salazar, who nodded and said, "Yes, Lope de Aguirre, he was one of them, but he also left a world full of Lope de Aguirres. When his body was quartered, it spread to the four directions of the Earth, and there is a piece of that madness in all of us."

Salazar was right. Gold fever had a paramount place in the discovery and conquest of the New World. It was the prime objective of the first voyages. Columbus found gold when his ship ran aground on Christmas Eve on the island of Española. At the sight of Indian gold, Columbus was pleased and did not doubt that gold among the natives implied the nearby presence of a gold mine. He wrote in his logbook: "I was very attentive to them, and strove to learn if they had any gold. I gathered from them that by going southward, there would be found a king who possessed great cups full of gold and in large quantities."[1] He built a fort of the remains of the ship and left for Spain with the news.

When Columbus returned to Haiti with many eager colonists, seduced by the stories of the golden lands, they found that the men he had left behind had made war on the natives and were dead, and the tiny fort had been destroyed. There was no gold mine on the island. The gold that they had initially encountered was alluvial gold that had been accumulating for eons. In order to have enough gold to send back to Spain, Columbus imposed a tax on the Indian population of the island to be paid in gold dust, and it proved impossible to meet. Columbus's imagination had invented the "incalculable gold" of the New World, but it was left to others to find it and fulfill the mariner's fantasy.

Colombia was named for this man who never set foot in the country. It was Alonso de Ojeda, one of his companions on his second voyage, who in 1499 landed at Cabo de Vela on the Guajira Peninsula. He briefly explored the Sierra Nevada of Santa Marta and was astonished by the wealth of the local Indians. This gold gave birth to the mysterious legend of El Dorado and imaginary gold mountains littered with emeralds.

According to the legend, the chief, El Dorado, went to the center of a great lake on a raft several times a year. He went naked, his body covered with gold dust. He would throw emeralds and pieces of gold into the water, chanting prayers. At the end of the ceremony, he would wash the gold off his body and into the water.

In recent times this legend was confirmed as fact. The leader of the Muisca Indians, who lived around the Laguna de Guatavita near Bogotá, would throw precious gifts into the lake from a ceremonial raft. The lake was formed from a giant meteorite some two thousand years ago. The Indians believed that the golden god lived at the bottom of the lake. The lagoon became an object of worship, and the offerings were to ensure the abundance of crops.

Over the years, many attempts were made to drain the Laguna de Guatavita to obtain the gold from the bottom. In 1545, Hernàn Pérez de Quesada, brother of the conquistador, attempted to drain it with a bucket chain of laborers. Antonio de Sepúlveda, a rich merchant of Bogotá, later cut a great notch in the rim of the lake, which lowered the level by twenty meters, until the cut collapsed and killed many of the laborers. In the 1800s, Alexander von Humboldt carefully calculated that one thousand pilgrims each throwing in five objects over a period of one hundred years should add up to some $300 million worth of gold at the bottom of the lake, in the currency of the time. Given those figures, the attempts to drain the lake continued.

In the 1800s, many attempts were made to drain the lake, and several sepulchers were opened, but mostly pottery and bones were found. In the 1900s, drilling equipment and steam shovels were used, but the lake resisted draining, presenting gold-seekers with dilemma after dilemma: extraordinarily soft mud, the same mud then baked by the sun to the consistency of cement, mud blocking the sluices. Although an amount of treasure was removed from the lake over the years, in 1965, the Colombian government finally brought the body of water under legal protection as part of the country's cultural heritage.

The conquest of the New World was marked by many stories of El Dorado that were sometimes real, sometimes illusory. From the beginning, this obsession with El Dorado was a principal force driving the Spaniards to the Americas and resulted in the rapid colonization of the country. The Spanish brought horses and cloth to exchange for gold and slaves. They pillaged the land of the Indians, directly or indirectly, looting their gold, their forests, their bodies, their religions, even their souls. Christianization was closely linked with the search for gold; it was both a force driving colonization and a tool facilitating it.

Columbus wrote in his journal: "Of gold is treasure made, and with it he who has it does as he wills in the world, and it even sends souls to Paradise."[2]

And Amerigo Vespucci wrote of the new land: "The trees are of such beauty and sweetness that we felt we were in an earthly paradise."[3] Many of the European arrivals called the New World a Garden of Eden—which, ironically, they proceeded to invade and destroy. In 1656, Antonio de León Pinelo wrote two volumes that sought quite seriously to demonstrate that the Garden of Eden was in America:

> In *El Paraiso en el Nuevo Mundo* (Paradise in the New World), he had a map of South America showing, in the center, the Garden of Eden watered by the Amazon, the Río de la Plata, the Orinoco, and the Magdalena. The forbidden fruit was the banana. The map showed the exact spot from which Noah's Ark took off at the time of the flood.[4]

We certainly ate of the forbidden fruit of the New World and released a flood of gold. In the first century and a half of conquest, one hundred eighty tons of gold and six thousand tons of silver was taken officially (more is thought to have gone unofficially) to Europe from the Spanish colonies in America. The gold greatly influenced the power structure of Europe. It was important to the growth of the first global empire—the Hapsburg Empire under Charles V, King of Spain, Ruler of the Holy Roman Empire, Emperor of the Indies. Sir Walter Raleigh said in 1596, in his writings on the search for El Dorado: "It is his Indian Golde that indaungereth and disturbeth all the nations of Europe. It purchaseth intelligence, creepeth into Councels, and setteth bound loyalty at liberty, in the greatest Monarchies of Europe."[5]

The gold brought back as masks, necklaces, crowns, nose rods, rings, pins, pots, statues, and other forms was melted down into neat gold bars. Gold was necessary to build new empires. It still is. Nothing has changed. Colombia still has a wealth of minerals that have not yet been exploited. The search for El Dorado continues today with all the corporate empires competing, primarily through their mining companies for exploration and "development" rights all over South America.

36

The history of the people in Western Colombia—and in Chocó particularly—revolves around gold. *Quebradas* (ravines) flowing with water from the Cordillera Occidental were the major gold-bearing streams of the Chocó region; almost every one contained gold. The Spaniards discovered the rich deposits and began to move into the area. They founded communities on the rivers where they located the mines, and they lived off fish, mollusks, and manatees from the streams and deer, tapir, and wild pigs from the forest. Travel to Chocó was difficult and dangerous, and only the promise of gold enticed them to the region that one early Spaniard described as "an abyss and horror of mountains, rivers, and marshes."[1]

Gold fever spread settlers throughout the Americas; it drove people to the far regions, to the untraveled lands, to places they believed to be flooded with gold. Population followed the rivers, the gold, and the supply routes, and new areas were colonized. Countless died in sickness, battle, and mining operations all over the New World in the search for the precious metal.

Some pockets of gold were discovered in Chocó, but mostly the gold was alluvial, and few shafts were dug in the area. The most common type of placer mining in Chocó was ground sluicing, which required many hours and many workers and for which slaves were commonly used. Robert Cooper West describes the process:

> A sluice channel, or *canelón*, is excavated along the base of a gravel bench to the depth of false bedrock (hardpan, *peña*), where the richest pay streaks are usually encountered. With iron bars *(barras)* the miners dig into the face of the bench, dumping paydirt into the sluice. Water is then run through the sluice and the finer materials are washed to the bottom of the sluice; large cobbles are thrown from the *canelón* with pairs of concave wooden plates *(cachos)*; next, the bottom of the sluice . . . is scraped with *almocafres,* short handled dibbles with hooked metal blades; a second washing ensues . . . and the precious metal is panned out with the *bateas* (gold pans). One sluicing operation . . . requires two weeks of labor by ten or fifteen workers.[2]

Open-pit placers were also common, using a primitive form of strip mining. Water was essential to the process; in the pit placers and ground sluices, huge amounts of earth had to be moved and washed to obtain the gold. As the region was quite wet, water was usually not a problem, but in some places reservoirs were used to store rain water.

Rain also swept gold from the earth into the rivers in Chocó. *Mazamorreros* panned gold directly from the rivers. The word *mazamorrero* meant independent prospector but probably had its origins in the word *mazmorra* (dungeon). Slaves were often forced to dive into the river's deep holes that served as nature's sluice boxes, catching heavy metals; the slaves gathered the gravel from the bottom and resurfaced hundreds of times a day. When the rivers were low, workers sometimes waded into the streams. William Sharp describes the dangerous process, which he witnessed even in 1976:

> Because the streams were very swift even when low, workers commonly tied large rocks to the small of their back to gain weight and stability against the current—a feat that requires exceptional balance. A slip in thigh-deep water with a large stone tied to one's back is hazardous. I witnessed this dangerous procedure on many occasions; it is still practiced by independent prospectors in the Chocó.[3]

Much gold was smuggled out of the region in exchange for "goods" smuggled in, such as slaves, rifles, and gunpowder. Mine owners wanted to avoid the *quinto* (fifth) payment to the Spanish Crown. The authorities attempted to control the contraband by closing the waterways into Chocó, limiting the number of ships entering. As they had to pass over sandbars at the mouth of the San Juan River, they could not be heavily laden. Stiff penalties were also imposed on people bringing in a mixture of metals. Platinum at the time was called *oro blanco* and was considered worthless. In 1720, Viceroy Jorge created a two thousand peso fine for a Spaniard mixing platinum with gold; any black or person of *inferior calidad* (inferior caste) would receive two hundred lashes.

Azogue (quicksilver or mercury) was used to separate the metals, but it was expensive. Given the heavier nature of yellow gold, a process of tapping the bottom of a tilted container could be used to separate the two weights; female slaves were most often used for the painstaking process because of their dexterity, care, and patience.[4]

Most settlements in Chocó were founded around gold mines without much thought given to the planning of towns. Initially, the indigenous people were used for labor in the mines, but their resistance and high death rate led the Spaniards to use Africans; gold was one of the main reasons they were brought to Colombia. There was also internal conflict regarding the treatment and conversion of the Indians, and early in the eighteenth century the use of Indians in the mines was outlawed by the Spanish. So miners shifted to the exclusive use of African slaves. By 1704, the Spanish had imported over six hundred slaves into Chocó. They used the Indians for other services, such as growing food and building houses for the miners and slaves and transporting people and materials.

The mines operated like huge machines built into the land, into which human beings were poured like fuel. When the slaves died, others could be rather cheaply rented or purchased. Eduardo Galeano, summed up the mines in the New World as sites where slaves were "used and scrapped. . . . In the places where they pan for gold, and in the galleries below ground, no black lasts ten years, but a handful of gold buys a new child, who is worth the same as a handful of salt or a whole hog."[5]

Indians in the area were organized into *corregimientos,* which were districts governed by a Crown official, a *corregidor.* They had their own *caciques* (chiefs) and *alcaldes* (mayors), but were under the control of the *corregidor* and had to pay tribute. The *corregidors* overworked the Indians, even using and renting them as *cargueros* (human packhorses). The officials monopolized food production, and mine owners had to pay the asking price to feed their slaves. The *corregimiento* system was profitable for the Spanish, and it provided the miners with food, but was annihilating for the Indians. The system had been set up to teach and convert the Indians, terms synonymous with exploitation in the New World. In 1808, Governor Carlos Ciaurriz made a lengthy report about the region. He stated that the Indians' lives revolved around superstition and witchcraft—they did not fear their sins; they never spoke the "sweet name of Jesus or Mary"; they recognized no difference between legitimate and illegitimate children; and they "experimented in love" before marriage. Furthermore, he made note that they believed every animal sound, whether the cry of the guaco bird or the roar of a tiger, to be an omen of things to come.

In 1820, after the Wars of Independence, Simon Bolivar prohibited the use of Indians without strictly regulated pay, and

Indians were no longer forced to live within specific settlements. Most dispersed to isolated regions and survived on subsistence agriculture.

Despite Bolivar's prohibition, however, Indians continued to be exploited, holding the most menial jobs. From the time of the earliest European arrival in the mountains and jungles of the New World, Indians and black slaves had been used as human packhorses, carrying up to two hundred pounds of gold, rubber, or other goods on their backs. They were even used to carry the Europeans themselves in *silleros* (chairs strapped to the men's backs). In 1824, Colonel Hamilton, appalled at the practice, wrote that the Europeans:

> mount these chairmen with as much sang froid as if they were getting on the backs of mules, and some brutal wretches have not hesitated to spur the flanks of these poor unfortunate men when they fancied they were not going fast enough.[6]

In the early 1900s in Colombia, peasants unable to pay their taxes because their subsistence agriculture left no surplus were forced to labor for the local authorities, acting sometimes as human packhorses. A law was presented to the Colombian Congress in 1916 to prohibit road tolls on people carrying goods on their shoulders, but it was not discussed due to its shameful implications.

Nearly a century later, on the Inca Trail to Machu Picchu in Peru, backpackers can still hire porters to carry their packs, and some even request the deluxe package—local porters not only carry the bags but also bring items such as a table and chairs strapped to their backs to set the travelers up for dinner. One almost expects to see people being carried up the trail in *silleros*.

37

THE EUROPEANS' ENCOUNTER with the natives of the New World posed a major ethical dilemma. Any and all action with respect to the native peoples had to be justified on the basis of the Europeans' own ethical code. This, at least in the early days of colonization, was predominantly the dogma of the Catholic Church. The interpretation and application of Catholicism had a profound effect on the relationship of Europeans with the Indians as well as with the Africans subsequently transported from Africa as slaves.

Bartolomé de las Casas, a Spanish Dominican missionary, also known as apostle to the American Indians, was among the first Europeans to recognize the implications of the discovery of America. Initially he supported Columbus and advocated the conversion of the Indians to Christianity. However, the terrible violence unleashed against the Indians and the injustice with which the *conquistadores* dealt with the natives turned Las Casas into an advocate for the Indians' cause. His *In Defense of the Indians,* which he published in the mid-1500s, exposed the barbarism of the colonizers and made a plea for the Indians to be treated as fellow human beings deserving of dignity and rights. He published anthropological works, such as the *Apologetic History* which disseminated a tremendous amount of information on the Indians in order to defend them from the charge that certain classes are inherently slaves. He did not judge them by Spanish or European standards but attempted to make sense of their beliefs within the framework of their own culture.

Men such as Juan Ginés de Sepúlveda, a contemporary of Las Casas, used Aristotle's theory of natural slavery to justify the barbarous actions in the new world. Drawing on Aristotle's theory, he declared unequivocally that some men are born to be natural slaves—*servi a natura.* They should hence be required to serve their natural lords, the Spaniards. Until the fifteenth century, Western Christians divided mankind on the basis not of race but of religion—whether they were fellow Christians or "infidels." Sepúlveda applied Aristotle's ideas beyond this distinction, stigmatizing an entire race as inferior. His works are considered the seed of the fierce racial prejudice that first took form in the New World. "Neither do they have written laws, but barbaric institutions and customs. They do not even have private property," Sepúlveda said. He considered the Indians childlike because they were willing to exchange valuable silver and gold for trifles. "The Indians are as inferior," Sepúlveda proclaimed, "as children are to adults, as women are to men."

Las Casas wrote arduously, trying to counter views such as Sepúlveda's almost as if in penance for his earlier advocacy of the Christianization of the Indians that had contributed to their enslavement and eventual destruction. However, in a time when slavery was a way of life, Las Casas also wrote a desperate proposal in his attempt to ease the burden on Indians in the New World. He said: " If necessary, white and black slaves can be brought from Castile." He later amended the proposal to "Negro slaves." Las Casas's views were respected by Church and Crown, and in 1518, two years after his proposal, Charles V first authorized the use of slaves in the Indies. Years later, confronted with the reality of the practice of slavery in America, Las Casas passionately reversed his position. In his *Historia,* he declared that "the same [natural] law applies equally to the

Negro as to the Indians." But the wheel had already been set in motion. One can hardly put sole blame on Las Casas for African slavery in the New World, but he did make a tragic mistake, and in this way he represents, perhaps, a common theme of human history. Even the best of intentions often set in motion events with unforeseeable consequences that can easily spin beyond our control.

It is unknown how many Indians lived in Chocó before the Spaniards came. Smallpox and measles epidemics in the 1500s ravaged the villages before a census was ever taken. In 1660, Jesuit missionaries estimated the number of Indians to be over sixty thousand; by 1778, only 5,414 remained in the central regions. By the end of the eighteenth century, Africans had replaced the Indians as the largest portion of the population. By 1782, they represented about two-thirds of the population. Some blacks recorded in the census were probably *mulatos* (black-white) or *zambos* (black-Indian). The census recorded only *blancos* (white), *indios* (Indians), *esclavos de varios colores* (slaves of various colors), and *libres de varios colores* (freedmen of various colors).

Libres presented an interesting question regarding race in Latin American society. In some countries, such as Brazil, mulattos had significant roles, and society was less divided than it was, for example, in the American South. In Chocó, for the most part, *libres* remained apart from whites in the society. There was a scarcity of white women, so miscegenation was common, but this did not bring acceptance of the *libres*. Spaniards in Chocó abided by the *limpieza de sangre* (purity of blood) doctrine. This doctrine had originated in Spain and had been used in the New World as an instrument to promote dominance of the Europeans. *Libres* had trouble finding work as there were no urban centers in Chocó. They had no rights to education. No school of any kind existed in the region until late in the eighteenth century, and that was created solely for the Indians. *Libres* were merely tolerated in Spanish society. Slave owners resented the haven such communities offered to runaway slaves.

Slave revolt and manumission (purchasing freedom) were common, and by the time of emancipation in 1851, only 1,725 slaves remained to be freed. Most of the blacks in Colombia lived in the San Juan and Chocó regions because of the extensive mining there. Very few blacks mixed with the Indians in this area. The Spanish attempted to keep the blacks and the Indians separate. They repeatedly prohibited blacks from living among the Indians, but of course this could not be completely enforced.

From the early years of conquest, the Spaniards considered all nonwhites simply as another "natural resource" to be exploited. This history of exploitation created a strict hierarchical system based on racial purity. This hierarchy is evident in the language itself.

Racial nomenclature in Colombia—and all of Latin America— is very different from that found in the United States. The North American system of classification by race is based on a historical distinction between white and nonwhite, exhibiting true racial prejudice. In Latin America, but not in the United States, racial classification involves many social factors and class distinctions that can blur and alter racial categories.

The great number of different terms used for racial classification shows that Latin Americans are keenly aware of race based on a variety of factors, particularly features such as skin color, nose shape, and type of hair. The nicknames that have arisen over the years, as well as accepted racial distinctions, are evidence of the effect of language working to create or maintain a social structure. The reality is that the multitude of racial terms in Latin America both reveal a fascinating history of the many combinations of people who formed the new world and also create a certain hierarchy based on racial characteristics.

Thomas Stephens's *Dictionary of Latin American Racial and Ethnic Terminology* has over 350 pages of words used for race and ethnicity. In Colombia alone, there are over fifty words used for racial classification, many of which carry in their definitions evidence of history and an element of judgment.

The racial categorization evident in the language was yet another outcome of the divisions created and sustained by the Spaniards in the New World. This divisiveness explains a great deal about indigenous and black relations to this day. The Emberá, for instance, have strict rules about race: only full Emberá are allowed to live in the village, and they prohibit marriage with blacks or whites. Salazar told me that one woman in his mother's village had been put in the stocks as punishment for having a black boyfriend in town. In Panama, I had asked an indigenous man from the Wounaan tribe about intermarriage between the Emberá and Wounaan, which he said was accepted, and then I innocently asked about intermarriage with people of other races. I received a very strong negative.

The isolated location of the province of Chocó and the history of exploitation of its land and people kept the communities divided, with no urban center for structure and social development. The repercussions of this can be seen in the lack of community between different ethnic groups today.

38

On my way to Colombia I had visited Ben, a geologist friend who worked for an American gold-mining company in Costa Rica. I found it interesting that he felt the need to justify his work to me; he kept extolling the virtues of his company, with its strong environmental department that "cleaned up" the land when it was finished extracting.

"Individual mining is far more destructive to the environment," he said. "They still use mercury to mine the gold."

"How does that work?" I asked.

"Well, mercury has a ready ability to link with certain metals like copper, zinc, or gold. It combines with all common metals except iron and platinum to form alloys called amalgams. Gold is extracted from the gravel by dissolving it in mercury. Then the mercury is removed by distillation."

"Where do they get the mercury?"

"It's been mined as well," he said. "It was the most lethal of mining in the New World."

Ben showed me a book on mercury which quoted Governor Juan de Solorzano in the early 1600s talking about the poisonous effects of mercury vapor: "The poison penetrated to the very marrow, debilitating all the members and causing a constant shaking, and the workers usually died within four years."

I remembered breaking a thermometer when I was little, and the small globules of the liquid metal rolled under the couch. When my mother found out, she had a fit and acted as though we would drop dead on the spot. She effectively scared us away from thermometers. Later I read about how mercury increases in concentration as it moves up the food chain, much like DDT, and how its use in the felt-hat industry and the mysterious symptoms that followed led to the origin of the term "mad hatter."

"Isn't mercury still used in so many products, like paint, and batteries, and the paper industry?" I asked.

"Well, yes," he paused. "but there's nothing we can do about that. My company, I mean. Like I said, we don't use mercury. And conditions of the mines in general are nothing like they were a few centuries ago, when millions of lives were lost to them. And the areas which were mined years ago were completely destroyed. They are deserts to this day. That's the difference between the way we mine today. We clean it all up; we fill the earth back in. And we usually just enter areas which have already been deforested."

"Usually?"

"Well, to be honest, occasionally, we are informed of a particularly rich vein we just can't pass up."

"Does your company ever mine on indigenous land?" I asked.

"Well," he said, pausing a minute. "Not usually. But it's legal. The government retains the mineral rights and sells them to the companies. If we didn't take the opportunity, someone else would. Basically, we try to make as small an impact as possible. And the locals welcome us. They get good-paying jobs."

"Until you move on."

"Until we move on," he agreed. "But sometimes they move with us."

Ben took me out into the field several hours northwest of San José, where they were testing for gold deposits. The nearby village was very poor and its people seemed glad to have the work the company brought in. The man who owned the land in question was an important person in the area and proud that gold had been found on his land. The company had been working with him, and there was a semblance of mutual satisfaction. But Ben confessed to me that the company was having problems with his "involvement" and was going to buy the land or close up shop and focus on a different area. It really did not like to deal with the requirements of the locals. I watched the man in his dealing with the geologists, his chest puffed out proudly, the gestures between them all smiles and arms around shoulders. It was hard to watch, knowing the "friendship" was soon to end.

I saw the core samples of the area, long tubes of rock punctured out of the earth from hundreds of meters underground. Ben ran his hand over them, picked up a piece, pointed at the marking which showed exactly how far down it was, then the rivulet of gold running through. The pattern in the rocks was beautiful, not one the same, layers of geological stories I wish I knew how to read. But Ben kept pointing to the stream of gold, the hair thin vein running through several of the tubes. "Not much, not much," he said, "but it's a good sign." He grabbed another piece and pointed out the gold.

I was still staring at the one in my hand, punched out from one hundred meters under the surface of the earth with some three-dimensional hole puncher. The gold looked like an underground river, running randomly and perfectly through the other "lesser" rock and mineral. I asked Ben where all this gold was headed.

"Well, it gets melted down into gold blocks kept in the company safe."

"And then?"

"I suppose to the next safe," he laughed. "A lot of this won't be used for quite a while. It's just a register of wealth."

I imagined safes all over the world filled with this precious metal of still somewhat mysterious origins. Scientists now believe that gold must have been created long before the creation of the earth. Any element heavier than iron must have been created by a supernova, which sprinkled it throughout this part of the universe.

Gold is hence the product of supernovas, as we ourselves are made up of the same basic elements as stars.

The sun had not yet fallen, but one of the first stars had already come out and beckoned there on the horizon. An invisible thread connected my eye to the star and the star to the rock in my hand, and I felt the little river of gold run into my own veins, reminding me that I too was part of this delicate balance.

39

[T]he voice of thy brother's blood crieth unto me from the
ground. And now art thou cursed from the earth, which
hath opened her mouth to receive thy brother's blood from
thy hand; When thou tillest the ground, it shall not
henceforth yield unto thee her strength; a fugitive and a
vagabond shalt thou be in the earth.

Genesis 4:10–12

As the traditional ways were lost and industrial agriculture
boomed in Colombia, a different form of slavery emerged. In
Miami I have seen the barges of bananas coming in through
Government Cut and have thought about the countries that
sent them, the "banana republics"—Honduras, Guatemala, El
Salvador, Dominican Republic, Panama, among others. The
history of the New World is reflected in the banana boat.

Early in this century, banana enclaves appeared in Central America
and influenced the agriculture, the industry, and the politics. The
United Fruit Company devoured its competitors, while its affiliates
took over the rails and the sea. The company took over the ports,
even setting up its own police; everything in Central America
revolved around the dollar. In *The 42nd Parallel,* John Dos Passos

comments about Minor Keith, the king of United Fruit, and the company's influence in the New World:

> In Europe and the United States people had started to eat bananas, so they cut down the jungles through Central America to plant bananas, and built railroads to haul the bananas, and every year more steamboats of the Great White Fleet steamed north loaded with bananas, and that is the history of the American empire in the Caribbean, and the Panama canal and the future Nicaragua canal and the marines and the battleships and the bayonets.[1]

In Colombia, United Fruit became the owner of the largest *latifundio* when a huge strike took place in 1928. Banana workers were massacred with bullets in front of a railroad station. It had been officially decreed: "The forces of public order are authorized to punish with the aid of appropriate weapons."[2]

The murder was erased from official memory. I first read of the banana massacre in Gabriel Garcia Marquez's *One Hundred Years of Solitude*. The workers made a series of demands relating to working conditions: the social security guaranteed by Colombian law, compliance with laws protecting workers in accidents, compliance with housing laws, the right to commerce rather than company stores, and the construction of hospitals. In the novel and in reality, the demands were the same.

The solution to the conflict is also identical in the historical and fictional accounts. The striking workers were declared "nonexistent." Technically, the company classified them as part-time employees, to avoid its legal obligations to full-time workers. When faced with the physical confrontation, the army massacred the strikers. History books vary as to the exact number of those who died; a telegram sent by the U.S. ambassador from Colombia to the State Department gave the number of deaths as over one thousand. In Marquez's novel, as well as in reality, there was complete silence regarding the horror; everyone feared the repercussions of speaking out. In the book, when Aureliano attempts to tell people of the train which carried the corpses away, he receives the response: "You must have been dreaming, the officers insisted."[3]

Eduardo Galeano sums up the history of the fruit in *Open Veins of Latin America:*

> The Koran mentions the banana among the trees of paradise, but the "bananization" of Guatemala, Honduras, Costa Rica, Panama, Colombia, and Ecuador suggests that it is a tree of Hell.[4]

Like bananas, coffee played an important role in Colombian history; it is often ranked on a par with oil in its importance on the international market. It is referred to as yet another "black gold" in this area's history. Coffee transformed the Colombian economy. Landowners and merchants made fortunes, and national markets and industries were created. Colombia, unlike much of Latin America, held onto much of the wealth from coffee production by maintaining a share of the trade, even when U.S. firms arrived in the 1920s. The National Federation of Coffee Growers (FEDERACAFE), established in 1927, kept Colombia in charge. The Colombian government owned most of the railway and coffee-husking plants.

In the 1940s, Colombian economist Luis Eduardo Nieto Arteta declared that coffee had achieved what mines and tobacco and other industries could not; a democracy of small coffee farmers had produced a stable and progressive order in Colombia. Unfortunately, he had spoken too soon; more violence was on the wing. For ten years, from 1948 to 1957, bloody conflict ravaged the country, leaving behind 180,000 dead. During these terrible years, the ruling class made a fortune, which made the country's economy look prosperous when, in fact, the poor became poorer or were massacred on the streets.

The story of coffee in Latin America reflects the absurdities of trade and investment relationships between First and Third

World countries. Galeano comments that "it is much more profitable to consume coffee than to produce it."[5] Sale and distribution of Latin American coffee provide countless American jobs, and coffee taxes end up primarily in First World coffers. The wealthy countries preaching free trade create stern protectionist policies against poor countries, imposing, for example, high taxes on their exports. Galeano states that instant coffee made in Brazil, for example, is better and cheaper than that made by the U.S. industry, "but then, of course, in a system of free competition, some are freer than others." He adds that the First World countries "turn everything they touch into gold for themselves and rubbish for others."[6]

In the twisted logic of trade and prices, natural disasters can become blessings for producing countries because they push up prices. But the collapse of prices after the 1929 crisis caused many Latin American countries to burn thousands of sacks of coffee, sending the hard work of so many farmers up in flames. The typical crisis in the colonial economy came from some outside influence.

Ironically, the consequences of rising prices can also cause economic trouble for producing countries. They lead to more sowing for more production, which creates an abundance of the product and brings down prices. In 1958, Colombia harvested the coffee sown with such anticipation four years before and had devastating losses because prices had collapsed. Colombia was so dependent on coffee and the external prices that historian Arrubla commented:

> In Antioquia, the marriage curve responds sensitively to the coffee-price curve. Par for the course in a dependent structure: even the propitious moment for a declaration of love on an Antioquian hillside is decided on the New York Stock Exchange.[7]

The landscape and agriculture of a region tell a distinct story about who and what has been exploited there. In his book *Middle Passage*, V. S. Naipaul talks about seeing the scars of slavery not only in present-day social relations but in the very vegetation of a region. He quotes Michael Swan from *The Marches of El Dorado,* who noted that "to force the Negroes of the Virgin Islands to work, the Danes cut down their soursop trees, and today in British Guiana, sugar must use a hundred subtle methods to maintain a sufficient labour force. . . ."[8] Naipaul also says he saw the evidence of exploitation:

> in the sugarcane, brought by Columbus on that second voyage when, to Queen Isabella's fury, he proposed the enslavement of the Amerindians. In the breadfruit, cheap slave food, three hundred trees of which were taken to St. Vincent by Captain Bligh in 1793 . . . so in Jamaica a clump of star-apple trees marks the site of a slave provision ground. (Trinidad, with only forty years of slavery, has proportionately far fewer star-apple trees than Jamaica.) There is slavery in the food, in the saltfish still beloved by the islanders. Slavery in the absence of family life, in the laughter in the cinema at films of German concentration camps, in the fondness for terms of racial abuse, in the physical brutality of strong to weak. . . .[9]

Our societies have developed ethics about owning another human being. We have established some laws to fight discrimination. We even have laws preventing mistreatment of some animals. Our laws reflect our changing attitudes. Yet our ethics are still forming in regard to most animals and certainly in regard to the Earth on which we live. In "The Land Ethic," Aldo Leopold opens his essay with a stark parallel:

> When God-like Odysseus returned from the wars in Troy, he hanged all on one rope a dozen slave-girls of his household whom he suspected of misbehavior during his absence.
>
> This hanging involved no question of propriety. The girls were property. The disposal of property was then, as now, a matter of expediency, not of right and wrong.

Concepts of right and wrong were not lacking from Odysseus' Greece: witness the fidelity of his wife through the long years before at last his black-prowed galleys clove the wine-dark seas for home. The ethical structure of that day covered wives, but had not yet been extended to human chattels. During the three thousand years which have elapsed, ethical criteria have been extended to many fields of conduct, with corresponding shrinkages in those judged by expediency only. . . .

There is as yet no ethic dealing with man's relation to the land and to the animals and plants which grow upon it. Land, like Odysseus' slave-girls, is still property. The land-relation is still strictly economic, entailing privileges, but not obligations.[10]

In our attitudes toward the land, one can see the history of our attitudes toward each other. We use it up, pollute it with waste and chemicals, discard it when it no longer serves us. Or we cut it into pieces, wipe out its origins, establish monocultures. What we are doing to the land, humans have done to each other throughout history.

40

One afternoon, while walking on the beach a few miles in the direction of Jurado, I almost stepped on a dead seagull, its body bent into something like an arrow pointing me down the beach. Ana Maria and I walked on and had cleared about twenty steps when a wave drew back and revealed another dead bird in the foam. We followed the trail, wondering what was killing them.

We came across a wooden construction where about five young men from Jurado were fishing. Ana Maria and I approached them to ask whether they knew anything about the gulls. But just as we reached them, one man caught what I first thought was a fish. He reeled it in, and I saw it was a seagull dangling from his line. He cursed, picked up a little club he had with his gear, and smashed the seagull with it a few times, yanked the hook out, re-baited, and threw his line back in the water, almost in one fluid motion. The seagull lay twitching on the ground.

Before I could even move forward, another man caught a seagull, damning it loudly as he pulled it in. Ana Maria ran forward. *"Espérate,"* she surprised the young man, telling him to wait and taking the line from him. She took the gull in her hands and laid it on the ground. She asked the boy to hold it still while she removed the hook. She opened its beak, and the gull didn't move, as if sensing the woman's intent. Ana Maria held the bird up in her hands and let it fly away.

As we stood transfixed, watching the bird for a moment, another man caught another gull, and Ana Maria went to rescue it too. This one was sick with pain, heaving and writhing under her hands. As she opened the bird's mouth, she realized the hook was down in the bird's belly and couldn't be removed. The men didn't want to cut the line and lose the hook, and the gull wouldn't have much chance anyway with a hook in its belly. Ana Maria stepped back, and we watched the man use the club a few decisive times, pull his hook from the blood and feathers, and wipe it with a cloth.

"It happens all the time," the man told us, pointing to the flock of birds hovering and circling the fishermen. "They're such stupid birds. They come down and steal the bait. *Basura.* Garbage birds," he finished.

I had taken some pictures of the past few minutes, of the spirit-lifting release of the one bird and the clubbing of the other two. Looking through the window of the camera, I had maintained a sort of distance from the situation, perhaps, but now, looking into the faces of the men, with the bloody birds lying all around us, I felt sick and sad, and the day was suddenly fiercely hot, the sun burning a hole in the back of my neck. To these men, the birds were garbage, cockroaches, pests that needed to be destroyed.

A few other men had come over to see what was happening with us—who these women were. When they heard the story and saw our stricken faces, some of them began to laugh. It was funny, anyone worrying about these garbage birds. A few of them thought it was kind of touching, ultrafeminine, perhaps, and had sympathetic looks on their faces—for us, not the birds.

I was to find many things in their rawest form on this journey in South America, from pollution, to sickness, to sexism. I have never been able to see merely the one situation, the men and the gulls. What I saw here was a product of socialization, a training that draws ethical lines and decides which species may live and which may die. It was a raw example of the anthropocentric attitude towards life that is inherent in North American culture as well. The difference is that in the States, we don't have to see it. We don't see the daily slaughter, drugging, and mistreatment of animals that make the essential meat in the average American meal. We don't see the chickens with their beaks and wings cut off, raised in tiny boxes in which they cannot turn around. We don't see the veal calves kept in darkness, chained in small wooden crates their entire short lives, kept anemic in order to produce light-colored meat. We don't see it. We don't know it. It is hidden in the Styrofoam and plastic wrapping at the supermarket.

Ana Maria and I left the fishermen, who were still laughing at our emotional response to the gulls. We walked a way down the beach, and I sat down, somewhat stunned by the images of the last half hour and by the connections they drew in my memory and my understanding of the world.

Ana Maria went down to the water. I noticed a couple of the young men had followed us and stood talking to her at the shore, then pointed to me a few times, then at her. I thought for a moment they might be talking about the pictures I had taken, that they wanted the film in my camera. Ana Maria had mentioned speaking to the mayor of the village about the gulls, and I wondered if they were worried about the evidence. But they left rather abruptly, and Ana Maria came back to the blanket.

"What were they saying," I asked her.

"You don't want to know."

"No, really, what did they want?"

She hesitated, "Well, if you must know, they were saying how cute they thought we were, and they wanted to know if we would come out to the disco with them tonight."

41

THE ENCOUNTER WITH the gulls and the men underscored the unalterable changes that Europeans had caused in the Americas, sometimes in the most peculiar ways.

Seagulls had a strange link to the exploitation of the New World. Since the earliest times, seagulls and pelicans, feeding on the prodigious schools of fish on the coast, had been dropping mountains of excrement rich in nitrogen, phosphates, ammonia, and alkaline salts. The value of guano as fertilizer had been discovered in Europe, where population had increased steeply and food production had exhausted the soil. In the New World, they discovered new "earth" in which to plant and moved literally mountains of it from one continent to the other. In the nineteenth century, guano was exported to European fields as a precious commodity, even serving as a guarantee for British loans. The exporters quickly plundered the fields; what nature had accumulated for millennia disappeared in a few years. Historian Robert Cushman Murphy wrote that:

the guano producers, long after the boom, were the world's most valuable birds in their dollar yield for each digestive process: they surpassed Shakespeare's nightingale that sang on Juliet's balcony, the dove that flew from Noah's ark, and, of course, the sad swallows of Gustavo Adolfo Bécquer.[1]

In the nitrate towns of South America, people thought the money would never stop flowing. Two-thirds of Chile's national income, for instance, came from nitrate exports. Yet it functioned, really, as only an appendage to the British economy. And when the Haber process of fixing nitrogen from the air was discovered in Europe, the New World's economy tumbled. The old nitrate towns became like ghost towns, left only with remnants of the nitrate railway lines, gaping holes in the earth, and slag piled up beside the excavations.

The pursuit of guano caused much bloodletting in South America in the 1800s over the rights to the guano fields. I had heard about the guano wars from a Peruvian in Cuzco, whose family wealth had been won and lost on the bird droppings. Peru did retain some deposits of guano, which, although there was no longer a great world market, remained the chief fertilizer for Peruvian agriculture. In 1960, however, the fish-meal boom destroyed the seagulls and pelicans that produced the guano. Fishing concerns, primarily from the United States, wiped out anchovy shoals near the coast to feed pigs and poultry. The birds followed the boats out to sea and, without the strength to fly back, fell into the ocean. Others stayed and scavenged in urban areas, often dying in the streets.

FIVE

Imágenes

1. Novenas in Jaqué

2. Ana Maria and Jaqué children

3. Ana Maria, Jaqué children, and the author, drawing stories in
the sand

4. Ricardo—between the forest and the sea, Chocó

5. Eusavio taking us across the river at high tide

6. Ricardo's house

7. Esmeralda, Alberto, Eusavio, and Ana Julia in the Gonzalo store

8. Seagull in Chocó

9. The Emberá village

10. Emberá children

11. Emberá canoe

12. Man loading mahogany, Jurado

13. Rain-forest wood

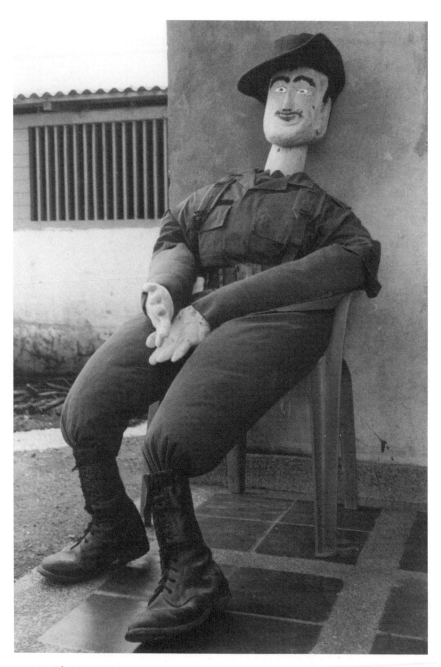

14. El Año Viejo

15. Children selling bananas

16. Neftali's boat

SIX

Dos Bocas

If you open the word "Basurame"
(turn me into garbage),
it becomes a command: love the south.

   —CECILIA VICUÑA,
     Unraveling Words and the Weaving of Water

42

A FEW DAYS before the New Year, we traveled to the Emberá village, Dos Bocas (Two Mouths), where Modesta, Ana Maria's Emberá friend, lived. The village was close to the place where two rivers converged, hence the name. The Emberá, like so many indigenous groups in South America, had lived in relative isolation in the Darién and Chocó forest for many centuries. They moved about the area by foot and by canoe, building transitory homes and villages. The Emberá were sometimes mistakenly called the Chocó Indians by earlier accounts, and there is very little recorded history about them. They presently inhabit the Darién of Panama and Chocó and Putumayo of Colombia and extend into Ecuador.

Dos Bocas was several hours upriver by motorized canoe. Along the way, we had to stop many times to wade with the boat, because the banks were eroding, the water becoming shallow, the trees falling into the river as a result of deforestation. Ana Maria had told me that until a few years ago one could travel straight up the river, even in the dry season. Now the mud, no longer held by the roots of trees, was filling the river with silt.

As we waded, I kept eyeing the water for snakes and leeches. When I asked about them, the boatman looked about in the water and said, "Sure there are snakes, but don't worry. Not all of them are poisonous." I wasn't reassured. Along the riverbank, piles of lumber were stacked in several places, waiting to be hauled to the lumberyard in Jurado. Some areas alongside the river had been completely destroyed; only stumps remained as far back as one could see.

On the other side of the river the land was still intact, and birds filled the canopy, some of which I recognized from having seen them in the Everglades: blue and white herons and egrets, clouds of them hanging on a single tree like ornaments. "Why are the trees only cut on one side?" I asked the boatman, Elio.

"I'm not sure," he answered. "Maybe they're just finishing with that side first." *Terminan* was the word he used, and in his statement, the terminal nature of the situation reverberated.

"You should be asking them your questions," Elio said, pointing to what looked like a barge which had just rounded the bend. He made a face and spat in the water. As the object drew closer, I realized it was not an actual boat, but merely several logs which had been tied together. "They're floating them down to the lumberyard in Jurado," he said. He deliberately looked the other way as the wood passed us, the men on board peering at the strange female cargo our canoe was carrying. We stared back, as another "raft" came around the corner, carrying another man with a pole, and then yet another followed in the grim regatta of makeshift vessels. "The Buenaventura boat must be in town," Elio explained. "Whenever it is, the men cut wood like crazy." He deliberately ignored the shouts from the passing men, as did we, as the procession very slowly and clumsily passed by us, bumping into the riverbank over and over with their unwieldy trees.

Particularly at the river bends, the water formed swirls that sucked the travelers to the edges. "They're being caught by the whirlpools," Elio said, "the *hëï*," he said in Emberá. "The river doesn't want to lose her trees, so she makes it particularly difficult to take them out."

As we reached the village, which was on the top of a steep, extremely muddy bank, several women and children came out to see us. Very few outsiders visited the village, and some of the children couldn't stop staring from behind their hands. Modesta waved from the top of the embankment and motioned us up, which, with all of our belongings, was easier waved than done.

Modesta was schooled in modern medicine. She wore modern clothes. She lived part-time in Jurado and partly in the village in a traditional house, which was built on stilts with no walls and a circular thatched roof. For stairs, there was a notched log known as a *tumé*. Most of the women in the village wore traditional dress: they were bare-breasted, with cloths, called wa or *paruma,* tied around the waist. Some of them used manufactured cloth, and some of the patterns came from the developed world. One woman wore a Star Wars pattern around her waist; another woman wore a cloth with Disney characters. Several of the women were painted with dark blue-black patterns covering their whole bodies. They used the juice from a forest fruit called *kipará* in Emberá or jagua in Spanish; the ink would remain on the skin for a few weeks. They painted themselves with the *jagua* to connect with the earth and sometimes to address a particular need—to ward off a sickness, for instance. One woman was painted so thickly that one could hardly see her body through the paint. Modesta said she was fighting off a bad illness.

Only full Emberá people were allowed to live in the village. Chocó is relatively isolated, and few Europeans ever settled there. The region of Chocó has some mixed-race individuals but is inhabited mainly by Emberá and descendants of African slaves, who have remained relatively unmixed compared to the rest of the New World. There were a few Indian children with blond hair. When I asked about them, Modesta said it was a nutritional deficiency, something I pretended to accept but wondered about quietly.

Most Colombians are of mixed race. As the history books might put it, the military conquest in the New World by European males, the initial scarcity of European women, and the widespread availability of Indian women led to the birth of many racially mixed babies. Modesta made a comment about the survival of the indigenous people, how the women had allowed themselves to be given children by their invaders in order to have at least some of their people survive. "Many of the tribes live on only through the mixed people," she said.

Yes, the genes were passed down, so some of the people did survive. Their strands of DNA reappeared in the next generations. The mixed faces represented the unions. But what did it mean in the hierarchy of power in the New World that so many of our mothers were slaves, that so many of our people were born of violation?

43

There were hardly any men in the village when we arrived—they were off cutting wood. The barge was in town in Jurado, and there would be good money for the trees that year. Only one man, Marcelino, came to the meeting we assembled that afternoon to discuss crafts. He wore the traditional garment of Emberá men, a loincloth known as a *me*. He farmed and was a craftsman and disagreed with the tree-cutting. Most of the people I had spoken to disagreed with the logging. But as the industrial world had moved in on them, particularly over the past twenty-five years, they had found it hard to keep up the old ways. They now needed money, and the trees were a source of it.

The proximity of Jurado was a problem for their people. "If the children go to school there, they never come back," Marcelino said. "I mean, their souls never come back. *Ése pueblo roba sus almas.* All they think of is money and drinking their money away. That barge in Jurado is a ship from Hell, and if I didn't value my life and my children, I'd set it on fire."

"But that wouldn't stop the logging," Modesta said. "They'd just send another boat from *El Norte.*" She was referring, I realized, to North America, conscious of the ultimate destination of the trees.

"The people want to go north along with the trees," Marcelino said. "It's hard to keep our children here. People are forgetting everything, how to harvest the fruits of the forests, how to carve a canoe, how to *plant,* if you can believe that."

I asked him to show me what he had planted this season, and he eagerly beckoned me to follow him out to his fields, which were just behind the village, while the people were assembling for the meeting.

Marcelino had been farming since he was a child and had planted *maiz* (corn), *boniato* (yams), *plàtano* (bananas), *pantrigua* (breadfruit), *guava, chocolate, café,* zapote (plum-like fruit), aguacate (avocado), and caimito (star-shaped purple fruit). I asked about the harvest, and he said the method depended on the crop. He said they would use a knife or sickle for the rice plants. They would make a special tool called the *azotadora* to remove the rice from the plants. The corn they would harvest one ear by one with knife or machete. Yams would be harvested in April or October. Bananas would take nine months, "like a baby," he added with an sudden smile. He had several of his children hanging on him at the time. Young children were allowed a greater freedom here and seemed somewhat spoiled by their parents. Ana Maria said it was just the way of the people; until the age of seven or so, children were given the run of the place and the run of the rules.

Marcelino had lost his parents and had been raised by his grandfather, who taught him the old ways. Most of the other young men had grown up in a changing village, in families in which the men left the village to work in Jurado or Buenaventura or a larger town and brought back the goods and values of the industrial world.

The people of this particular village still rejected plastic, but Ana Maria told me that in Jurado, as in many Third World villages, plastic had become a sign of status. The people who had moved to Jurado looked at the things of the modern world much as we have been trained to—as progress. They wanted to buy industrially produced goods. They began to use materials like nylon instead of natural fibers. They learned to receive store-bought products wrapped in plastic bags, which, ironically, indicated luxury and wealth.

All around the edges of the river from Jurado to the Emberá village, plastic bags blew around, cans and bottles lay discarded, and the people left them as if they now formed part of the landscape.

When Ana Maria and I returned for the gathering with the village women and Marcelino, we discussed the possibility of developing crafts from the natural products of the forest, for export as an alternative source of money. The villagers had brought woven baskets, bracelets, necklaces, and carved figures to show us. The baskets were dyed with juices from berries and leaves and had intricately woven designs and animal shapes; they used a palm they called the *pärärä* to do the braiding. The bracelets and necklaces were intricate in beadwork, and Modesta told me that the Emberá wore the beads around their necks to ward off evil.

Some women wore as many as twenty necklaces at a time. The large beads were *kirrima,* and the small ones they called *neta.* The wooden figures were children's toys mostly, likenesses of themselves and creatures of the forest and the sea. They also carved images in the seed of the tagua tree, which Ana Maria called vegetable ivory. The carvings were white and smooth; we looked at a snake, a frog, a dolphin. One woman, Elena, saw me admiring a horse she had carved within a large white seed and gestured that I should take it as a gift. *"Es tuyo,"* she said, telling me it was already mine. Ana Maria said I should accept it and find her a gift later among my own things.

We spoke with the people about marketing and exporting their work. Ana Maria explained that it was a small operation but could provide a reasonable flow of income—more, anyway, than the slave wages for the tree-cutting—and the grassroots group she was working with wanted only products that came from renewable sources. She told them that people back home valued such artwork, and many people valued knowing the source of the item. There was a certain kind of consumer who would deliberately choose products that came with an assurance that no people, animals, or landscape had been exploited in their production. When we mentioned that people back home would pay about ten dollars for each carved piece, for instance, the villagers seemed almost incredulous. "For one toy?" one woman asked. "You can live for weeks on that." They leaned forward, eagerly pulling more pieces out of their baskets.

Ana Maria, via her grassroots group, had arranged for products to be exported from other villages, and she wanted to begin the process here to offer another option. Money had been unnecessary in the self-sustained village fifty years ago. People gardened and hunted and raised some animals. But the new generation, no matter how isolated, had already become rather reliant on the things of the modern world. They had already been affected by industrial civilization, and Ana Maria wanted them to receive their fair share.

Marcelino said they would bring up our offer in the large meeting of several local villages to be held in a few days. Armando Achito, Modesta's brother, was an important figure in another village downriver and would be hosting the meeting. His village was also the intended destination of the microscopes we had brought with us.

As we discussed matters with the people, I thought again about how abruptly things had changed here. It was symbolic of the extraordinarily rapid change that had taken place since the Industrial Revolution—in just a few generations—and it made me think of my own grandmother, who reused and recycled everything she could. She grew herbs and vegetables even on her balcony when she lived in an apartment. She threw nothing away—she saved every jar, every container, every toilet-paper roll. She once built an incredible dollhouse for my sister and me, completely from materials others would discard. She made a baby's crib for the dollhouse from the top of a detergent bottle and the bottom of a bottle of dish soap. She covered everything with scraps of cloth she had left over from dresses and bedclothes she had made.

But many of those values got lost in my parent's generation as the majority of people left the land behind. In the 1950s, the great era of atomic testing and lethal pesticides, my parents became adults. They grew up in an era that built against nature—suburbs, cookie-cutter houses, lawns, and landfills became the norm, and with the loss of diversity in the natural world came the decrease in diversity of lifestyles. As television moved into every household, people all over the United States watched the same shows and received the same messages. My mother told me about the pesticide companies' propaganda in the fifties. Anyone opposed to widespread pesticide use was actually labeled anti-American, even a communist. The DDT vans drove through the neighborhoods spraying lawns and houses once a month. Most people accepted it as the new order of things and didn't question the dangers.

Both of my parents had grown up in rural areas, my father in Europe, my mother in America. But part of success in the modern world is to obtain the means to leave the work of the land to others. In that process, a schism occurs between humans and the natural world—nature is viewed as something outside us, something belonging to another dimension.

44

I HAD BEEN feeling "nature's call" at the village for about three hours before I finally said something. Modesta called a little girl and told her to take me out to the place. The child took my hand and began to lead me. About seven other little girls came with us, as if it were some exciting excursion. They were dressed in miniature skirts resembling their mothers' and no shirts. They had beads around their necks, and a few had their bodies painted elaborately. We walked along the cliff and down a path to the river, passing many circular huts along the way. Laundry flapped on the clotheslines and on the branches of trees behind the houses, and I noticed several old canoes up on stilts. They appeared to have plants growing in them. I asked one little girl what they were, but she shyly hid behind her older sister, about eight years old, who said, "She doesn't speak Spanish. Only Emberá."

She seemed surprised at my question about the plants inside the boats. "They are gardens," she said matter-of-factly.

"Why are they up on stilts?" I asked.

She looked at the other girls and then back at me, confused, as if anyone should know the answer to that question, and said, "To keep the animals from eating the garden." The girls laughed a little among themselves, and then suddenly the little group stopped. I had imagined we were going to some kind of outhouse, but they had stopped a little way up from the river-bank and the leader pointed down the embankment. I looked.

"*Donde?*" I asked after a moment. The girl giggled and pointed again. I was still unsure of the procedure and where exactly she wanted me to go, but I went down the riverbank and, trying not to think about what the mud I was sinking into might contain, pulled down my pants and squatted. All the little girls stood at the edge and watched me, still giggling.

Something was making them laugh. As I shifted uncomfort-ably, I began to laugh myself, feeling the absurdity of my situ-ation and having bizarre thoughts about etiquette, about guest towels. I knew that these girls, who had never left the village, never seen a bathroom, must have thought it was pretty funny that I didn't know how to conduct myself properly. Did I go too far down the riverbank? Was I supposed to take off my pants and go into the river?

I finished my business, rinsed my hands in the river, and struggled back up the bank, to the little line of witnesses, still giggling into their hands.

45

THE FOLLOWING DAY, Modesta and Marcelino took Ana Maria and me into the forest to point out some of the wild plants and fruits. They both knew the folk biology of the forest, and Modesta, having spent time in the city, made a joke about the river being their refrigerator and the forest their drugstore. She said she thought it was unfortunate, though, that so many of the young generation had no interest in learning the stories of the plants. She blamed it on Jurado and other towns like it. "Once they go to Jurado," she said, "all they can think about is soda and candy, radio and TV. They have a TV there now, you know."

Many of the people resisted sending their children to the school in town, although many felt it was a necessity in the changing world. Many had forgotten the forest, had forgotten the old ways, had begun to think of education as something you received in a school in town, in Spanish or even English if you truly wanted to achieve, to make progress. "But you can learn everything in the forest," she said. "It is the true school. It is where we learn all our 'subjects'—our biology, our medicine, our history, our stories. It is where you can see how everything works together, how one thing is connected to the next. You can see the history of every plant in the direction in which it grows, read the stories in the way they wind around each other." Her words made sense to me. I had been trying to come to terms with the fact that not much of my urban environment made sense for the continuation of our existence.

Much of the problem lies in education, in what and how we are taught. Most people have knowledge in the very limited area of their specializations. Hardly anyone could sustain himself or herself if the present structure of society broke down. How many people today have ever grown food? Who knows the first thing about the basic necessities for survival?

I said to Modesta, "Back home, learning takes place in separate little. . . ." The word in Spanish for classroom escaped my mind, and I paused for a moment and then said, *"en cajitas,"* which I meant as classrooms but which is actually the word for "little boxes." Modesta and Marcelino nodded—they understood completely.

"So here is your biology lesson . . ." Modesta said, "out of the little box. Since my daughter is off hiding with her friends somewhere, you can be the replacement for today." She laughed when she spoke about her daughter, but I felt the seriousness under her voice about the fate of her daughter and her people, who had resisted assimilation for so many centuries. As we walked into the trees, I felt the temperature lower by several degrees. I began to list the forest in my book as they named things, mostly using the Spanish words although sometimes using the Emberá equivalent. I knew instinctively that I would never find an English equivalent for some of the names. Modesta showed me the *trupa,* which I already knew, and the *corozo,* both of which would be harvested in February or March. She said they drank the juice for health, and they also took oil and pomade for the skin from them. She pointed out *cajetajo, churirra, dozzarejo, jensrajo,* and *borojo,* which were all good nutrition. I had tried *borojo* juice several times with Ricardo; it was a bittersweet, maroon-colored liquid unlike

anything I had ever tasted and which grew on me after the first
sip. I started to crave it after that, so much so that I wondered
about the full extent of its properties.

In addition to her training in Western medicine, Modesta
also knew the medicinal value of the forest plants. She picked
kidabe leaf for me to chew on, saying it was good for preventing cavities. She pointed out the *hombregrande* (bigman) and
the *jagua* fruit, the juice of which I had seen on the people's
bodies. She said that they used it not only for religious ceremonies but for allergies and some infections. *Korata* was useful
for nausea and vomiting and any sickness caused by parasites.
Paiko would be mixed with *cogollo de mostenco* (homeless
shoot) for parasites as well. She bent down and dug up a small
root which she called *raizilla*, which was used to induce vomiting. She gathered some of the other herbs and plants in a basket
for her "medicine cabinet," as she called it.

Marcelino named the trees for me and told me how the
people traditionally used each of them. They would use a
variety of different woods for the foundation of the houses:
*caoba, cedro, roble, kira, laurel, espinosa, cedro espinosa,
jira,* or *chunga.* The thatched roofs they made with *palmas de
wágara, palma real, potorrico, platanillo,* and *corozo.* He said
certain trees were used specifically for the building of boats: the
kalkolí (wild cashew tree), *pino amarillo* (yellow pine), *espave,
espinoso,* and *cedro.* He pointed out a few others that he said
they didn't really use: *guayakil, ceibo, matapalo,* and *higueron.*
He said they used the fruits of the *nënzarahö* (star apple),
makenke, michilá, jéapa, and *tagua* for their subsistence. He
called the familiar rubber tree the *huéporo* and said they used
the sap for various purposes.

I asked Marcelino about hunting, and he said he didn't usually hunt—he was more of a farmer—but that, traditionally,
the people hunted *conejo* (rabbit), *begí* or *venado* (deer), *mono*
(monkey), *ardilla* (squirrel), *tapir, armadillo, ñeque, saíno,*
and reptiles such as the turtle. The animals of the forest that
they did not eat were the *imamá* (jaguar), *puma, tigre congo,
tigrillo,* and others such as the *oso caballo* (horse bear), *wánga-*

nos, laardilla, chidima, gotutú, bichichí, gato perezoso, jojomá, oso chaqueta, cusumbí, and *marteja.* He said they also did not eat reptiles such as the *serpientes venenosas y no venenosas* (poisonous and nonpoisonous snakes), *cocodrilos,* and *largatos* or amphibians such as toads and frogs.

He said they mostly ate fish when they could get it: *pargo rojo* (red snapper), *moná* (a kind of sawfish), *sardina grande* (large sardine), *macana* (club), *sábalo* (shad), *mecedora* (rocker), *doncella* (maiden), *bailarín* (dancer), *baú* (catfish), *abalete, chongorro, pez agujeta, cangrejo, maikuika, pejeperro, chogorrita, conchudo, burá, pichimarra, guacuco, bocuna, pemá, sojorro, machipila, charre, jinchirú, buchi, bitunsi,* and *korromá.*

I asked about the birds of the area, and he rattled off a long list. He said they ate *pavas* (turkeys), *loros* (parrots), *pavones* (peacocks), *kewará* or *tocanes* (toucans), *guacamayos* (macaws), and *paisanas,* and then listed others that, he said, filled the forest with their voices: *águilas* (eagles), *gavilánes* (sparrow hawks), *buhós* (eagle owls), *buitres* (vultures), *palomas rabiblancas* (kinds of pigeons or doves), *pericos* (parakeets), *cóndores* (condors), *colibrís* (hummingbirds), *tautaus, lorqueras, perromulatos, palomas torcazas, condornizes, chingués,* and *tricas.*

As he was listing the birds, occasionally a call of one would echo through the trees, and he would give the call an owner and a name. I thought about the way our knowledge affects our senses, how we see what we know. I remembered taking a hike in the Everglades with a group of biologists who named all the trees and the birds and the insects as we passed them. I thought about how much I must miss every time I pass through a place like this, because of my limited knowledge, my limited sight.

Annie Dillard says that "the lover can see, and the knowledgeable." We pass through our environments and see what we know and what we believe. Conversely, what we don't know, we never see, and it becomes as if nonexistent.

46

There are hundreds of crossroads in the grass-moor.
A stranger like you can easily go astray.
This horse knows the way.

—Matsuo Basho

We slept that night, as we had the night before, in Modesta's hut under mosquito netting. We arose at four in the morning and, loading up microscopes, water pump, and books, left immediately to walk to the village where Modesta's brother Armando Achito lived. The way was difficult through the forest which, even though it was dry season, was wet and muddy. The sun was not yet up, and the morning had that otherworldly quality of light—perhaps it was partly the sleep still in my eyes, but it was also a hazy predawn fog that had not yet lifted. Even the trees seemed to hang still and heavy with the weight of the night still upon them. As I blinked the cloud from my eyes, I half-expected to see some little people of the forest still engaged in the night's festivities.

Modesta said we were going to a very important meeting to discuss the New Year; decisions would be made about the land, the water, and the tree-cutting. Usually, such meetings were closed to all outsiders, but the people knew and trusted

Ana Maria, and as her companion I would also be welcome. Modesta told us her brother would be very happy to see the microscopes, which would be helpful in diagnosing and preventing illnesses. His small son had been very sick with cholera because he had drunk unboiled water from the river. And many of their people had been ill at least once with malaria. They would have a healing ceremony that night for Armando's son. Another brother walked with us carrying the ritual boat he had carved for the ceremony. I had seen Modesta the night before carving a face on a figure by candlelight. She said it represented an ancestor and that others were also bringing figures.

"They are the ancestral spirits which will travel from the spirit world to take part in the healing ceremony," she said. "The ancestors will arrive in the boat my brother built."

One of the men walking with us, Loremiro, told us that we would be welcome at the ceremony and could add our prayers to the healing. He was the shaman of the two villages and had spent the night before carving a ceremonial prayer staff. It was four hands long, he said, because four was a magical number.

I asked him how he had become a shaman, and after waiting a moment as if unsure whether to answer, he responded at length. It surprised me a bit, since many questions I had asked people had been answered with one word. He used two words interchangeably for shaman: brujo in Spanish, and *häïmbaná* in Emberá.

"You become a shaman after having endured crisis where you see spirits or are possessed by spirits. In order to be cured, you follow, accept the spirit into you, and become shaman," he said. "Anyone can become shaman, man or woman. But you must undergo the encounter in the other world. You must recognize your teacher. I wish my grandson to be shaman when he grows older, but this is not certain. He will inherit my staffs, and the animal spirits within them. I will be his teacher, but there is always the chance he will not recognize me in my other form."

I asked him what he meant by that, but he merely shook his head and continued, "To be shaman, you must learn the songs. You must learn to fill the songs with power—sing them with power, and over many years and many visits with spirits and other shamans, you may acquire vision. It is not merely the words themselves that you must learn, but how to sing them. They will help you learn to discern between good and evil intentions. That which appears good may be rotten inside; that which appears bad may be full of sweetness. At the end of your body's life, you may finally have learned to fill the song to its capacity."

Someone near the head of our party called his name, and Loremiro went on ahead, very swiftly for a man of his age. We moved quickly through the forest, the Emberá stepping easily through the same brush that grabbed me in its long fingers, leaping lightly over the same mud that sucked me in, once or twice even up to my knees. We traveled for about three hours. I didn't know how far it would be, and I didn't have the time or the breath to ask, so I just kept moving forward without questioning. In my experience, three hours was a long time to move without stopping, and I could feel myself dragging. Ana Maria didn't seem to have much trouble; she was keeping pace with Modesta near the front of the procession. I had fallen to the very rear of the party and stopped momentarily to take a breath, dislodge my foot from a muddy root, and wipe something from my eye. I looked up. The people were gone. I stared around the thicket that seemed to have formed around me, searching for a sign of the right direction. But the leaves were still and seemed untouched by any travelers.

"They must have rounded a corner," I thought, feeling a small moment of panic. But the forest just seemed to have closed around them. A slight wind had begun and the trees shook their leaves as if they were laughing. "They must be right up ahead, and if not, they'll come back for me," I kept saying to myself. But logic is often lost on a heart beating fast.

At that moment, I heard a sound from the underbrush, the loud rustling of a very large animal. Images of tigers and pumas and mythological beasts flooded my head. I remembered Ricardo's warning about the tiger roaming about in early morning. I might have screamed, but my voice wouldn't leave my throat.

The forest beside me suddenly opened up. I swallowed and blinked my eyes. Out of the trees stepped a huge white horse directly in front of me, shaking its head free of leaves. It paused a foot away and looked me in the eye for a long moment. I almost expected it to speak, but the horse turned then and moved through a small break in the trees on the other side that had been invisible to my untrained eye. I followed. Not more than twenty feet away was a clearing, and the round roofs of the Indian village appeared in the sunlight as if they had just materialized. I looked back for the horse, but it had disappeared somewhere back into the forest.

47

In European accounts of the New World, the sentiment is heard again and again: "After God, we owe the victory to the horses." For indigenous people, however, horses as a symbol had a poignant duality. They represented the conquerors, and yet they were the one gift from the Old World that became a valued and significant part of indigenous culture. The truth of human affairs is always mixed: a dark spot in the light and a light spot in the dark.

Horses ranged widely in the Americas over ten thousand years ago when large numbers of humans crossed the Bering Strait and arrived in the New World during the last Ice Age. With the changes in climate and flora, invading parasites, and the arrival of Paleo-Indian hunters, many species of large mammals in the Americas were made extinct: mammoths, giant ground sloths, mastodons, giant buffalo, and horses, for instance. Homo sapiens, expanding into the Americas, found the land full of huge herbivores inexperienced in defending themselves against humans. They proceeded to enjoy these great blessings of seemingly inexhaustible sources of protein. Alfred Crosby comments in *Ecological Imperialism*:

The Americas and Australia were Edens to which God added Adam and Eve very tardily. "There can be no repetition of this." wrote François Bordes in *The Old Stone Age,* "until man lands on a hospitable planet belonging to another star."[1]

After the ice caps had melted and the oceans had risen to their present levels, the humans were isolated in their new world with a host of new species. In a sense, horses were among the truest native Americans but became extinct on that continent some eight to ten thousand years ago. The horse *(Equus caballus)* survived, however, on the Siberian side of the Bering Strait and ranged throughout Asia and Europe. Some six thousand years ago, the first ancestors of the domestic horse were captured from the wild horse population in Eastern Europe. They were used for charioteering and riding by the eighth century B.C. and later for cavalry and lance horsemanship, which spread throughout the continent.

The horse was viewed as a magnificent figure in many early writings. The Book of Job says of the horse, "the glory of his nostrils is terrible. He paweth in the valley, and rejoiceth in his strength: he goeth on to meet the armed men. He mocketh at fear, and is not affrighted; neither turneth he back from the sword." And God asks of Job, "Hast thou given the horse strength? hast thou clothed his neck with thunder?" (Job 39:19–22)

Perhaps man did not create and clothe the horse's neck with thunder, but he did something remarkable and symbolic of human's existence on Earth: he tamed the horse. A millennium later, Sophocles declared one of man's great accomplishments to be the taming of "the wild horse windy-maned."[2] We clothed the horse's neck with bit, bridle, and reins. And thousands of years later, our modern-day reality of genetic engineering even threatens to answer God's question about creation in the affirmative.

Iberian horses were the ones first introduced in the New World by the Spanish. The most significant event in the history of Iberian horse breeding was the Roman invasion of Iberia in the late second century B.C. The Romans brought their Oriental stallions and used them on the indigenous mares. This was the world's first attempt at crossbreeding domestic horses. The cross brought the surprising results of four new traits thought of today as typical of American horses: large size, short speed, good gait, and contrast in coat patterns.

The Spanish horses became known as the finest in the world for combat. These were the horses Columbus brought on his second voyage, which were bred in the Caribbean and then brought to the North American continent. Hernando Cortés, Francisco Pizarro, and other *conquistadores* imported horses from the islands to aid in military ventures. Pizarro also imported some directly from Spain, and horses spread quickly in the lush valleys of Peru. The animals spread throughout the Americas as swiftly as the conquerors. In some areas, such as the tropical areas of the Caribbean and Central America, the horse was slow to propagate, but in others, such as the pampas of the Rio de la Plata in Argentina, the horse found the perfect habitat.

The story of the horse is symbolic of human conditions in the New World, evident in Eduardo Galeano's description of the sacrifice of maverick horses in the 1700s. He wrote:

> Peons bring these wild horses to the corrals mixed in with domesticated ones, and there they halter them and take them out one by one into open country. Then they turn them over and with a single slash, open their bellies. The mavericks still gallop, treading on their entrails, until they roll on the grass; and the next day dawns on bones whitened by dogs.
>
> The wild horses wander through the pampa in troops that are more like shoals, flying fish slithering between air and grass, and spread their contagion among the domesticated horses.[3]

In 1541, Pedro de Mendoza is said to have abandoned a few mares and stallions when he fled the starvation of his colonists in the Argentine Pampas. The horses were joined by feral stock from Tucumán and by horses escaping through the Andes from Chile. The feral mustangs were known as *llaneros* or *baguales,* or in Mexico, as *mesteños* (which North Americans corrupted into "mustangs"). At the beginning of the seventeenth century, when the first permanent population settled Buenos Aires, Vasquez de Espinosa wrote of the pampas as being overrun with "escaped mares and horses in such numbers that when they go anywhere they look like woods from a distance." He wrote that the wild horses "cover the face of the earth, and when they cross the road it is necessary for travellers to wait and let them pass, for a whole day or more, so as not to let them carry off tame stock with them."[4]

Horses spread north as a result of Spanish settlement, trade, Indians escaping slavery, and capture from tribes still unconquered. By the middle of the seventeenth century, the Utes and other indigenous tribes were using horses. In 1777, Friar Antonio Morfi wrote that the Rio Grande area contained so many horses that "their trails make the country, utterly uninhabited by people, look as if it were the most populated in the world."[5] Thomas Falkner, the Jesuit, recorded the prodigious numbers of horses on the pampa in the eighteenth century and the going price of half a dollar a head. He wrote:

> They go from place to place, against the current of the winds. . . . Sometimes they passed by me, in thick troops, on full speed, for two or three hours together; during which time, it was with great difficulty that I and the four Indians, who accompanied me on this occasion, preserved ourselves from being run over and trampled to pieces by them.[6]

Ranchers regarded feral horses as pests because they ate grass and competed with cattle. Fences were often used not to keep horses and other livestock penned in but to keep them out. Wild stallions were a particular nuisance, often impregnating valuable mares. In some places in the New World, in seven-

---

teenth-century Pennsylvania, for instance, anyone who found a stallion "under thirteen hands running free had the legal right to geld him on the spot."[7] Whole herds of horses were often seen as such pests that they were destroyed like bugs:

> When the gold rush began in 1849, there were so many wild horses that ate so much of the grass that livestock-men with an eye for the profit that other stock could make out of the same grass drove the horses off the cliffs at Santa Barbara by the thousands.[8]

Even today, thousands of feral horses still run free in the western parts of North America, despite blizzard, drought, and the pet-food industry. Free-roaming horses in such numbers have existed nowhere outside the Americas for many centuries. Their great abundance on the plains of North and South America was a major factor in shaping both societies, but particularly that of the pampas:

> more firmly and more permanently than the discovery of gold would have. The metal would not have lasted long. The enormous herds of wild horses, the indispensable element of *gaucho* [cowboy] culture, lasted for two and a half centuries.[9]

When the horse had been domesticated thousands of years before, it was an accomplishment as transforming as the discovery of fire. The horse represented the rapid change that took place in the world, its pace escalating through the millennia. Although machines largely took over the functions of the horse following the Industrial Revolution, language still reflects the horse's vital importance to human history. The "iron horse" changed the landscape and the very concept of distance. Even today, the more successful of machines earn the title "workhorse," and we measure the capacity of engines in "horsepower."

Indigenous cultures in the Americas were forever changed by the cloven-hoofed invaders, as was the very ecology of the hemisphere. The importation of six species of hoofed mammals—cattle, sheep, goats, hogs, asses, and horses—had a visible effect on areas in which they were introduced. Horses found it particularly easy to assume the old ecological niche they had enjoyed ten thousand years before. Settled native peoples found the horses problematic in their lands, as they rooted up, ate, and ran over their farms and stocks of seeds. The Native Americans were forced to adapt to the presence of these new beasts and assimilate them into their cultures. Like the rest of the world, they learned to harness the power that horses brought—for travel, speed, and warfare.

The horse became the Native American symbol for the journey, but not merely a journey of this world—it was also a symbol for remembering the journey of our ancestors. A frequent historical Native American statement was "Stealing horses is stealing power." This often meant both physical power and unearthly power, as many cultures incorporated the horse into their mythology. Horses were thought to enable shamans to fly through air to heaven. One Native American story tells of the shaman Dreamwalker's encounter with White Stallion, who was the message-carrier for all other horses and represented wisdom in power. This magnificent horse was the embodiment of the balanced medicine shield. Dreamwalker, the shaman, was healed by the visit of the wild horses.

48

With the white horse and centuries of history in my head, I entered the second Emberá village, where all the different Emberá communities were gathering to discuss policies for the New Year. The conversation was often difficult to understand. The people spoke in Spanish but occasionally lapsed into their native tongue, particularly at heated moments. We were introduced as friends and welcomed by the people, although somewhat coolly, I thought. I realized later that what I often took for coldness was mostly a question of cultures. I was raised in a culture of smiles and polite exchanges, phatic remarks to encourage a speaker to continue. A speaker in this culture would be greeted with a stony face and often no remarks or gestures to urge one to continue.

It was close to noon, and I was very hungry after such a long morning hike with no breakfast and hardly any dinner the night before. Marcelino's wife had prepared us a special dinner of *guagua*, a gopher-like animal which the Emberá raised in cages under their houses. I had been introduced to them that afternoon, and I hadn't expected one to end up on my plate that evening. At first I couldn't identify the mysterious food on my plate, until I noticed a small claw sticking out of the batter on someone else's plate. Realizing I really wouldn't be able to get this down, I pretended a few bites and secretly handed the rest to one of Modesta's daughters, who had been given only a finger-sized leg and had been eyeing my generous portion.

There was also an unidentifiable fried dish on the plate which I asked about, wondering if it were meat. "No, it's not meat," was the answer. I took a small bite. It was soft but a little chewy. Perhaps it was some kind of mushroom. I asked again, but they kept using a Spanish word with which I was not familiar: *tripa*. But they kept adding the words, "not meat." Finally, one woman pointed to her stomach and made a circling motion with her hand; it finally dawned on me that I was eating intestines, probably of the *guagua*, no less.

I had been served the dish of honor, and Ana Maria, seeing my sudden realization and horror, secretly and quite generously swept the patty onto her plate and ate it down in a few bites. I blessed her for the favor. "Not meat." It made me think of my father, who knows I haven't eaten red meat for years but still offers me items like liverwurst and sausage when I visit. He does not think of them as meat, probably because much of our food comes in a form we no longer recognize as having been part of an animal.

The next day, given the small portion of dinner that had actually ended up in my stomach the night before, I was particularly hungry, and as we joined the circle forming in the hut, I found myself eyeing a woman chewing on a piece of coconut. I was thankful when a few minutes later a woman, Selena, brought us cups of an herb tea and some bread, which we ate rather quickly. The tea was quite delicious, soothing, with a slight taste of licorice. I asked her what it was, but she only replied, "A special mixture—for travelers." When I asked again, she said, "It's good—good for travelers."

Ana Maria leaned over and said to me, "She doesn't want to part with her secret recipe." I wasn't sure whether or not she was joking. Selena did ask us if we would like some more, and

I readily accepted and ate another generous helping, thinking the tea and bread was the lunch. I was still hungry, though, so when a young girl came back with bowls of soup, I again accepted heartily. It was a thick, delicious, root-vegetable soup with carrots, yuca, potatoes, and plantains. Ana Maria and I both finished ours quickly. The young girl returned, and seeing us scraping the last of the bowls, asked if we would like another. I looked at Ana Maria, wondering whether taking another bowl would be proper. Ana Maria pointed out the huge pot over the fire. So we accepted another bowl, grateful for such a generous lunch.

One can imagine our embarrassment when the girl then returned with full plates of the main course—rice and fish and bananas—and handed us each a plate. I really could not eat another bite. I wondered what they must have thought of us as we ate a whole loaf of bread and then two big bowls of soup. I had to refuse my plate, explaining how full I already was.

Despite my embarrassment, I found the situation quite funny. I felt like my dog back home who eagerly raised her ears every time someone stood up, wondering whether she was going for a walk, or followed us into the kitchen thinking she might get some food. She was never certain what to expect. And she couldn't ask.

49

WE PRESENTED THE water pump and microscopes Modesta had asked us to bring. They needed the pump mostly for irrigation, especially during the dry season. They brought water into the village in buckets from the river or used collected rainfall. Malaria was a serious problem in the area, and they needed the microscopes to detect disease and be able to treat it. There was no electricity to power the light, so Modesta would have to use sunlight to see by. The people gathered around, investigating the new devices, each taking a turn peering through the eyepiece at dust, a hair, a fingernail before the meeting began.

The children were given free rein, wandering through the circle, sitting on one lap and then another, playing with pens, or the dogs, or someone's hair or shoelaces. If one of them became cranky, the mother might pull the child to her breast, even children who seemed as old as three years. Armando's little boy, the one sick with cholera, was in particularly bad spirits.

I had noticed signs painted on the huts in Modesta's village: *"Tome agua hervida"* (Drink boiled water). Years ago, people used the river for everything without worry: cooking, washing, drinking, and the fast flow kept the water clean. Conditions had changed with all the toxic chemicals, unsanitary disposal of waste, and population growth in the nearby town.

Cholera had not been a concern in this village until recently, when it was brought on by deteriorating water quality and the epidemic that was sweeping the continent at the time. Both cholera and malaria are diseases associated with water. Water, which had been hailed by all ancient civilizations as the bearer of life, was also feared as the bearer of death. Monsters of the swampland were feared in many cultures in Africa, India, and Scandinavia. The well-known Greek myth has Hercules battle the Hydra, dweller of swamps and springs. For each head cut off, two new ones immediately appeared.

Throughout the world, malarial conditions in swampy areas have for millennia incapacitated whole armies. The same disease that killed Alexander the Great also killed the poet Lord Byron in Greece in 1824, two thousand years later. In the 1800s on the island of Corsica, 80 percent of the male population was unfit for military service due to malaria; in British Guiana, as much as 80 percent of the garrison was attacked yearly by the disease. It is no wonder, then, given the scourge of this disease and its places of origin, that the words "swamp" and "marsh" still have such negative connotations in our language, despite the rich ecosystems they contain. The negative association comes from a basic fear for survival.

In 1956, the World Health Organization (WHO) began a campaign to rid the world of malaria and with the use of DDT, dieldrin, and other measures effectively eliminated malaria in the United States, most of Europe, Israel, and Cyprus by 1978. But even before Rachel Carson's exposé of the long-term dangers of DDT (in *Silent Spring*), many recognized that DDT could be used only in limited areas, as widespread use destroyed all the insects of a beneficial nature as well as the parasite-bearing mosquitoes. In some parts of the world, such as Central America, mosquitoes became resistant to DDT and other insecticides, and some parasites were resistant to anti-malarial drugs. In 1946, for example, only two species of the

Anopheles mosquito were resistant to DDT; by 1976, forty-two species were resistant to dieldrin, and twenty-one species were resistant to DDT and dieldrin. Widespread use of pesticides in agriculture sped up the development of resistant populations of mosquitoes.

Millions of people around the world still die annually from malaria. In fact, disturbing rises in the disease have occurred in recent years. There have even been cases of locally acquired malaria reported in the United States in recent years. As malaria is a disease of the tropics, some scientists think the rise in cases of the disease is an effect of global warming, as malaria mosquitoes have been recorded as being able to survive farther north and in much higher elevations than before.

Malaria (bad air) is recorded in writings from ancient times. Malaria fought off those who attempted to invade ancient Rome far better than the inhabitants' weapons could. Hippocrates described the disease in great detail and thought it was nature's way of delivering the body from "corrupt matter." Although the effects of malaria were recognized, the causative agent was not discovered until close to the end of the nineteenth century.

Amerindians in Peru at the beginning of the seventeenth century were already using the bark of the fever-bark tree as a cure for malaria. In typical imperialist fashion, however, the fact that the Indians knew the property of this tree and were using it for medicinal purposes was discounted in most accounts, as when, for instance, Sir George Baker wrote in 1785: "a casual experience of an uncivilized people."[1]

The treatment was given to the countess of Chinchon, wife of the Spanish viceroy in Peru in 1629, and the tree was subsequently named *Chinchona*. The countess took some of the bark back to Spain, and the tree was established in India, Ceylon, and the East Indies. In 1820, the French chemist Pelletier extracted the alkaloid quinine, the most important active principal in the bark, and thereafter quinine was used to treat malaria. Although folklore in several parts of the world linked malaria and mosquitoes, this fact was not proven until the end of the nineteenth century by Ronald Ross.

Control of malaria today attempts to address environmental conditions. Malaria flourishes in a temperature of 65 to 85 degrees Fahrenheit and in a humidity of 60 to 70 percent or above. Usually, wet conditions allow the malaria mosquito to thrive, but a steady flow of water in a river can flush out larvae and pupae and serve as mosquito control. A condition of drought, ironically, can actually increase malarial conditions as rivers dry up and shallow pools form which are good breeding grounds for the mosquito. Other approaches to mosquito control involve genetic solutions—releasing, for instance, sterile males into the environment or introducing pathogens such as bacteria that are harmful to the mosquitoes.

In developing countries, malaria still poses the same threat as it did fifty years ago—and possibly a greater one. Some of the reasons for this are pesticide-resistant mosquitoes and the fact that present methods of control, while effective in one area, are not suitable for other conditions. In many Third World countries, the effects of invasions, political unrest, civil wars, and unstable economies have much to do with the spread of disease.

The people in these remote regions do not have the most basic of health services. We brought the microscopes as a personal donation. They were necessary to diagnose malaria and prescribe the proper drug. With malaria, the usual treatment, chloroquin, is also used for prevention. I had been taking chloroquin tablets, but as a preventive method, chloroquin is meant to be taken for only short periods of time, or it would wreak havoc on the liver. It is not a solution for the people here, who have to live with the threat of the disease daily. Education about the diseases is a key factor. Many of the people do not necessarily understand the science of cholera or malaria, but they now know not to drink river water. They have learned not to let water stand in basins for mosquito larvae to accumulate. These are things they have to take more seriously with a changing environment, with a river that is slowing down and drying up. Worsening environmental conditions are turning the threat of sickness such as malaria, which had always been a matter for some worry, into the most serious of concerns.

Cholera was not a widespread problem in the Americas in the twentieth century until it suddenly reached epidemic proportions in January 1991. The epidemic was first reported in Peru and spread quickly throughout South America.

Cholera is an old disease that induced terror on a scale similar to the scourge of the Black Death in the Middle Ages. Diarrheal diseases have been recorded since the earliest of times: "And thou shalt have great sickness by disease of thy bowels, until thy bowels fall out by reason of the sickness day by day" (2 Chronicles 21:15). Cholera is caused by the bacterium *Vibrio cholerae;* the bowels turn to water and cannot hold fluids or solids. If untreated, those infected will die of dehydration, demineralization, and dealkalinization. Cholera victims are usually clear of mind but have a terrible fear of impending death, as they quickly wither away without a means of replenishing their bodily fluids. In 1831, the French doctor François Magendie wrote a description of the disease:

> A person in the best of health, when he is smitten by the cholera, is in an instant transformed into a corpse! There is the same state of the eyes, the same aspect of the face; the same coldness of the limbs; the same colour of the skin, etc. Were there not the intelligence left, so to speak, intact, were there not a remnant of the voice even though almost imperceptible, one would proceed to burial at the actual moment of attack . . . to put it all in one word, the disease which is under my eyes in an instant cadaverizes the person whom it attacks.[2]

It is small wonder the disease has such a swift effect, considering that the human body is primarily water and that our bodies die within days without water.

Cholera was always thought to be transferred from person to person, but the outbreak of the 1990s seems to have been a very different beast. Biologist Rita Colwell spent years fighting popular belief and amassing evidence that bacteria and viruses lurked inside algae. Her premise suggested that the oceans have become great carriers of the disease. Due to raw sewage, pesticides, fertilizers, and other chemical waste, algal blooms have increased in frequency. Global climate change is warming the oceans which are already filled with the wastes of various nations, and this is compounding the danger. As oceanographer Patricia Tester commented, "The oceans have become nothing but giant cesspools, and you know what happens when you heat up a cesspool."[3]

In the 1970s, Colwell believed and subsequently proved that the cholera vibrio could live dormant inside algae for months, perhaps even years. Lab experiments mimicked changing environmental conditions: as nitrogen and temperature were increased and salinity decreased, the cholera awoke from within the algae.

The epidemic in South America is believed to have come from bilge water brought from the Asian Sea and released into a Peru harbor in the very hot January of 1991, made hotter by the effects of El Niño. Cholera then spread quickly throughout the continent, often straight into people's homes, pouring from their water faucets. By January 1994, millions of Latin Americans had fallen ill with cholera and thousands died.

The most vulnerable to disease are the poor in the festering cities and in remote communities with relatively few treatment facilities. Coastal communities, whose people live by the tides of the rivers and the oceans, now deal with the reality of poisoned water washing into their homes.

Existing cholera vaccines cannot be used for the control of the epidemic because they do not prevent transmission of this strain of cholera. At the time of our visit, new vaccines were being studied, but treatment involved oral rehydration salts, intravenous fluids, and antibiotics flown into remote regions, as well as educational programs to slow the spread of the disease. Modesta said it had taken several deaths before medicines had arrived in Jurado, and it was still a task to get them out to the remote regions. Cholera acts swiftly and fiercely; once it steals the waters of the body, death is only a question of time.

The World Health Organization admits that environmental devastation is a major cause of the spread of new diseases. Global warming, altering wind patterns, and changing levels of relative humidity and rainfall could radically alter the ecologies of microbes carried by insects. It has brought and will continue to bring microbe-carrying animals into closer contact with humans. Heightened exposure to ultraviolet light also has the effect of breaking down the immune system. Even in developed countries, we can be affected by these changes. Global warming and the fact that we have cut down so many of our trees (nature's air conditioners) heighten reliance on artificial air conditioners in our cities and recirculation of microbe-polluted air. Thousands of cases of "sick building syndrome" have been reported in the last few years.

While attempting to eradicate disease, science has also created new avenues for it to travel. We have awakened the cholera sleeping within the algae and spread it throughout this continent. We are creating more and more favorable conditions for malaria to spread; in the words of Rachel Carson, "the insect enemy has been made stronger by our efforts. Even worse, we may have destroyed our very means of fighting."[4] We have altered ecosystems dramatically and in many cases have eradicated natural systems of purification. And in the jet age, disease has yet another way to travel. A person can leave the bush and be in the States several hours later, serving as a host to any number of highly contagious, even fatal diseases. In our efforts toward progress, we have both created and beckoned new diseases out of the oceans and the jungles and into other parts of the world.

50

Water, as our lifeblood, has risen to the top of ecological considerations everywhere, but it is often not addressed until it becomes a life-threatening problem. In the words of the American folk song by William Bell, "You don't miss your water till your well runs dry." In the United States, we are absolutely reliant on an elaborate system of artificial purification of water. Back home in South Florida, for instance, the construction of canals and years of agricultural runoff have destroyed the flow of water and the marshes that naturally cleanse and purify it. The old saying that "water flows uphill towards money" still applies.

For decades in Florida, water has been rerouted for agricultural purposes such as "Big Sugar"; the Everglades, deprived of their natural ebb and flow, have been almost completely destroyed in the process. And much of the water is wasted. Instead of being allowed to flood the ground and have time to seep into the aquifers, rainwater is often channeled directly into the ocean. The precious fluid is lost, and even in South Florida's wet climate, we now find ourselves with water shortages. As

South Florida expands at a furious rate, we can only expect much more significant shortages in the future.

In the United States, we depend on machines and bottles for our water, for everything. As a culture, we have no sense of the source of things or their life spans. We buy a soda, drink it down in a few minutes, and leave an artifact behind. We flush our toilets, put our garbage out on the curb, and everything magically disappears. It may disappear from sight, but it fills our landscape with trash and pollutes our waters. In the Emberá Third World village, I could see my own world reflected much more clearly. I could see the reality of the conditions which my own world treats, chlorinates, and disguises within its landfills.

I could also see my own world reflected in the struggle for power between the indigenous villages and the black people of Jurado, the *libres*. The people of African heritage in Chocó, struggling for basic survival themselves, received a bit more education and privilege in Colombian society than the indigenous people. They often took advantage of the only group "below" them in the hierarchy of power. Relations between the races had been particularly strained in the last few years. Armando told me the story of what had occurred recently to open the rift even further.

"There was an argument about the land upriver," he said. "We never felt the need to claim it because we just moved through it on our way to the "farms" and between the villages. But now the trees are like money—green, like your money in the North," he said to me. "The people in Jurado think that having a chain saw means having a right to the trees. And the Emberá are cutting them too. It's as if the ones who can cut them fastest are the true owners."

He pointed in the direction of Playa de los Muertos. "That beach had its name before the man was found dead last year. He was a tree poacher from Jurado, one of the first to come with a chain saw. Before long, it was ten chain saws, and ten men working for him. Some of our young men spoke to him one day in the center of town. I was there to stop them from killing each other. And another time they almost did battle on the barge, where they were bringing the wood to be shipped out. That man was near death his whole life, that's the only way I can put it, he had so many enemies. Every man who worked for him—Emberá or *libre*—hated him. He hired out the chain saws and charged such rent that the people brought home only their drunken selves when they were done with the week. Anyone might have killed that man. But when he was found dead on the edge of the cut forest, lying over the stump of an old tree, of course they thought it was one of us, an Emberá, who did the killing. And maybe it was—no one will admit to it, and I can't say for sure. But no one knows what happened to the man's hands, or how there was so much blood. His hands were chopped off and when he was found the next morning, all the blood had already left his body. The land was red with blood. It had splashed the tree stumps, and after he fell, it had run down from his wrists, as far as the river, and probably even emptied into the ocean."

51

THOUGH THEY WERE not termed as such, environmental questions were sensitive issues and high on the agenda for the meeting. In a place like this, it was not a question of saving something separate—the environment was not an "other" but something they felt in their very bodies, in their daily movements. The babies got sick when they swallowed the river, the trees were all disappearing, the riverbank was eroding daily, and the canoes couldn't make it to the next village. The people were beginning to realize how dire the situation was because they were living the changes.

After a few hours of discussion, we were given *chicha*, prepared for the occasion. Traditionally, chicha was prepared in the following fashion: several people chewed maize or sugarcane and then spat it out into a large pot. The mixture was then fermented for several weeks. Usually the maize chicha was used for ceremonies, and the more potent sugarcane alcohol was for parties and celebrations. A modern version of chicha had existed for a while, without the chewing, but in the small villages they still prepared chicha for ceremonious occasions in the traditional manner.

On the previous day in Modesta's village, Modesta's daughter had been sent for chicha. She left once, then returned and got some red dye from a red fruit she called *achiote* to put on her hands and face—to "protect her from the spirits," she said. She had returned empty-handed, saying she'd been unable to get it, and wouldn't explain further. Modesta then asked one of the women to go, and she brought back a *totumba,* a gourd full of the liquid, which we drank. I had taken a tiny cautious sip, worried somewhat about the chicha-making process and somewhat about the spirits.

This day's chicha seemed thinner, possibly produced with more modern methods, but how could one know? In Punta Ardita, I had found a small worm swimming in the drink, after I had already drunk half of it, so I couldn't help but be squeamish. Here, one bowl was passed around the room. I drank my portion and said a silent prayer for health.

After debating the issues brought up for several hours, the people reached agreement on a few matters. Almost all were interested in marketing their crafts, and Ana Maria arranged to pick the crafts up in a month on her way back through the area. She left a deposit of several hundred dollars with Modesta and Armando, who would be in charge of distribution among the villagers.

The tree-cutting was an issue that caused greater dissent. Many of the young men at the meeting felt that the tree-cutting had become a necessity in order to survive in the changing world. They spoke of immediate economic matters. Loremiro countered their comments; he made statements about being one with the forest, that this tree-cutting, then, was like suicide. He said the forest would know what was being done and would retaliate. Food would disappear, the river would dry up completely. "It is all connected," he said. "The forest is like a brain. And it is far smarter than we are being."

When Armando Achito stood and spoke at the end, he spoke for the majority. The hut became suddenly quiet, as he announced one of the decisions: in the New Year they would cut no more trees for the barges in Jurado. They could not police the whole forest, but at least on the land between the villages and farms, they would stop the cutting.

"If we erase the forest, we will no longer exist," he said. "Even our ancestors will have no way to travel back. And if we lose our previous generations, we lose our future ones too."

52

When I asked questions, I tried to get the answers down in my notebook like any good interviewer. I had stopped asking people how to spell things when I realized that often they had no idea. I wanted to get the correct record, but I realized that some words were purely regional, some purely oral. I had received interesting reactions to my writing down what people said. Ana Maria had asked me not to write during the big meeting at the village because it made the people less likely to speak their minds if they had fear of the information being captured.

I remembered reading about the dream symbolism of various indigenous people, that to dream of papers was a sign that the dreamer was going to encounter a white man, and that some legal misfortune would take place. Michael Taussig, in *Shamanism, Colonialism, and the Wild Man* comments that "the magic of the printed word as print has acquired this power in the exercise of colonial domination with its fetishization of print, as in the Bible and the law."[1]

Eduardo Galeano refers to a decree issued in 1908 that represented the power of the written word to make or erase anything, even an entire people:

The governor, General Miguel Marino Torralvo, issues the order for the oil companies operating on the Colombian coast. *The Indians do not exist,* the governor certifies before a notary and witnesses. Three years ago, Law No. 1905/55, approved in Bogotá by the National Congress, established that Indians did not exist in San Andrés de Sotavento and other Indian communities where oil had suddenly spurted from the ground. Now the governor merely confirms the law. If the Indians existed, they would be illegal. Thus they are consigned to the cemetery or exile.[2]

Papers certainly have power in our society, whether they be identification, legal, or political papers. Perhaps the reliance on papers is at the root of the problem. In B. Traven's book *The Rebellion of the Hanged,* the revolutionary schoolteacher in Chiapas, Mexico, says:

If you want us to win and stay winners we'll have to burn all the papers. Many revolutions have started and then failed simply because papers weren't burned as they should have been. The first thing we must do is attack the registry and burn the papers, all the papers with seals and signatures—deeds, birth and death and marriage certificates. . . . Then nobody will know who he is, what he's called, who was his father, and what his father had. We'll be the heirs because nobody will be able to prove the contrary. What do we want with birth certificates. . . . I've read a mountain of books. I've read all that's been written about revolutions, uprisings, and mutinies. I've read all that the people in other countries have done when they become fed up with their exploiters. But with regard to burning papers I have read nothing. That's not written in any book. I discovered that in my own head.[3]

Actually, though, Traven was just advocating the methods the conquerors had used in the New World in burning what existed. Only four Mayan hieroglyphic books out of hundreds remained after the bonfires of Christian missionaries, who aimed to destroy every example of traditional Mayan belief. Luckily, however, Mayan scribes, fluent in Spanish, secretly encoded traditional Mayan knowledge into the language of their conquerors in books such as the one known as *Popol Vuh*. The actual title of the book in Mayan is the *Pop Wuj*. *Popol* has no significance in the Mayan language, while Pop refers to the woven grass mats knelt upon in ceremonies. The crossed web of fibers represent thought and understanding. *Pop Wuj* means a book of science and wisdom.

Thinking of the Mayans, my pen suddenly felt like another symbol of the developed world, the world that wrote the history down, with all its gaps, one-sided perspectives, and direct lies. I felt its great capacity for evil weigh in my hand. Yet at the same time, I recognized its power to transform, to make things happen, to awaken sleeping giants that might need waking.

53

I TOLD LOREMIRO that I had been keeping in my book a list of Emberá words I had learned, and he asked to see them. I gave him my book tentatively, wondering whether I had written anything down that I shouldn't have. He looked at the list and began shaking his head. I was about to apologize when he held out his hand for my pen. He proceeded to correct the words, adding accents or extra letters. "Why are you collecting the words," he asked. "What are you going to do with them?"

They're for poems, I answered, not sure what to say. "Your words sound like songs. I want to remember them when I am back home."

He nodded, handing me back my book. "Words are like spells *(brujeria),*" he said. "They have the capacity to heal. But they can also kill. You must consider carefully every word you use. You will use them to return here someday." I looked down at the page where he had added the word *hëinene.* "Now that word is a whole poem," he pointed with a long finger. "It is the tree that burst open to form all the world's rivers. The wild cashew tree. In Ancient Times, Woodpecker and Horned Lizard were stealing water from the tree. Ankore [God] knew and asked them where they got the water. They refused to say, and Ankore got angry and burst the tree open. The water washed the people away, and each branch of the tree became a river. That word you will never forget."

achiote: red fruit used as paint for ceremonies (Spanish)
algorobo: hard fruit with fuzzy-covered seeds in the center
ambugé: bench by the hearth; shaman's bench for rituals
Ankore: God
Antumiá: demonic messenger of shaman
begí: deer
besia: stay
bicho: creature, parasite
cacique: chief
canto: song (Spanish); also used by the Emberá to refer to the healing ritual as a whole
chibigi: turtle
chicha: fermented corn drink; ritual shaman's song
chicharra: dragonfly
chikwé: crab
comarca: reserve
creciente: rising current, flood (Spanish)
daú: eye
daúbaráda: shaman
detripando: removing the innards
diablito: little devil, spirit (Spanish)
doedá: river
doté: canoe pole
eyábida: unmarried indigenous person
guarapo: fermented sugarcane drink
hai: animal spirit(s), familiar(s)
häïmbaná: shaman
hamará: basket with straight sides and large mouth
hampá: canoe
häüre: spirit
hëï: whirlpool
hëïmaneto: girl's rites of puberty

hëïnene: mythical tree which broke open to form the
world's rivers

hirua-numua: illness; caught in fire of devil-spirit

huéporo: rubber tree

imamá: jaguar

iña-bákara numua: illness; inability to breathe

itarra: hearth; fire

iwá: hallucinogenic vine (Datura)

jagua: black dye from fruit of Genipa americana

kalkolí: wild cashew tree (Anacardium excelsum); wood
used for canoes

kampuniá: nonindigenous person

kau: daughter

kirrima: large beads

kugurú: large pot

makenke: firewood

makwá: vine used as rope/love potion

me: loincloth

mohópono: balsa

nënzarahö: star apple

neta: small beads

pärärä: palm used for basketry

pepena: woven fan for the fire

pidókera: hardwood used for the house posts

raizilla: root used for emetic

so: heart, character

so-droma: angry-hearted

so-pua: in pain

sukula: sweet banana drink

tadzi: I/we

tamarinbó: tamarind

trumpa: courtship with music

tuétahö: guava fruit

tumé: notched log used as stairs for houses

üchuburrï: little baskets with round bottoms and
narrow tops

umatipa: high noon

ürähó: honey
wa: wraparound skirt (Spanish: paruma)
wëra: woman

That night the people gathered to be painted for the healing ceremony, and some, for the following day's journey to Quibdo. There was another meeting of various indigenous tribes to be held in Quibdo, the capital of Chocó, and Ana Maria had been planning to join them. They would leave the next morning by motorboat, and I would be going back alone. Some of the people were going into Jurado for supplies and for the New Year's parties, and the plan was for me to travel back down the river to the dock in Jurado to catch the motorboat to Jaqué.

Ana Maria had asked for us to be painted as well. It was not really a good idea to wear the *jagua* in Jurado or Jaqué, so she said they wouldn't paint my face. They said the paint was to protect me for the journey home and to keep me connected to the forest but that I should wear it under my clothes. "How long will it last?" I wanted to know.

"Two weeks," Ana Maria said. "Or one day, or forever. It depends," she laughed. "No, two weeks. It stays on your skin for two weeks."

We went into the hut with several other women; the sun was already setting, so they had candles ready. Some girls came in with carved gourds half-filled with blue-black paint. One of them handed her mother, Isme, a small instrument made from bamboo, a flat three-pronged paintbrush.

Isme told me the *jagua* was used for various purposes: people wore it in preparation for danger, it connected them to the land, and it was often used for spiritual purification, sometimes after a wrongdoing. The person would also sometimes be washed with another plant called *kerápachi (albaca),* would have to eat meat without salt, and would eat a specially prepared *plátano* which would have been wrapped in a leaf for seven days.

I had noticed some of the children painted with *jagua,* and Modesta had told me that one or two of them had been sick and that the paint was for medicinal purposes. "It's good for the skin," she said. "It purifies you inside and out."

Ana Maria took off her blouse, and after pausing a moment, I started to remove mine, but she laughed and said, "Wait, I'll be first." I watched as the women began to paint her with long strokes of the bamboo sticks. They started at her shoulders, her back, and her chest. Three women were painting her at the same time, and I leaned forward to see the designs. The brushes made three strokes when laid flat. I asked one of the women what the designs were, and she answered, *"Culebra"* (snake), and described another one on Ana Maria's back as the Creator, or Earth Mother.

I watched mesmerized by the now-flickering candle and the women painting Ana Maria's whole body from her neck to her waist and then her legs. The room was sometimes silent and sometimes filled with the music of their language when they discussed the next stroke of paint.

When Ana Maria was finished she stepped away, and some other women began to fan her with woven fans. The paint would take a while to dry, and she had to be careful not to smudge the designs.

A little nervous, I removed my shirt, hiked up my skirt, and stepped into the circle of women. One of them laughed at the look on my face and promised me that it wouldn't hurt.

Then they became serious again. The brushstrokes began all at once in three places on my body—my chest, my shoulder, and my back. Each stroke of the bamboo felt like a cat's tongue against my skin.

They said they were doing the same designs as they had on Ana Maria, but they were going to give me more of the earth, less of the *culebra*, because I was younger, because I was here for the first time, and because I would be returning home soon. The paint would connect me to the place even as I traveled on.

They painted the earth pattern down each of my arms, one long stroke down and then short strokes coming out of the sides. It looked like I had trees on my arms. I said so, and Ana

Maria smiled. "That is what I said the first time. I felt like I was being turned into a tree by their brushes."

I closed my eyes and felt my limbs begin to grow. My feet became roots suddenly, stretching down into the damp ground, and burrowed home. I raised my arms so they could paint my sides, and I felt them extend upwards and burst into branches. I could imagine the tip of every one blossoming with a bouquet of flowers, open to the bees and the sky.

The women began to fan me, and I knew that they had finished. I opened my eyes and looked down at my painted body, felt the cool breeze of the fans like the wind through the trees and knew that even after I moved, my roots would stay here like memory and forever connect me to this moment and this place.

We walked through the dark, the wind finishing the process of drying the paint on our skin. The child's house had been prepared for the healing ceremony. Some of the Emberá, like Modesta, had learned modern medicine, and the tribe accepted some of the gifts of the other world. They saw our microscopes, for instance, as tools with which to identify better the cause of sickness. Loremiro had thanked us for the powerful *daú,* the eye that we had brought from the other world. I had learned that *daúbaráda,* from the root for eye, was another word for shaman in their language. The Emberá had begun to incorporate the two forms of healing. The boy was being treated with antibiotics, yet he would also receive the ritual healing of the shaman. They now believed that the two forces combined would be what brought the child back to health.

The women had brought sweet-smelling leaves and spread them throughout the hut. They had removed all animal spirits and banished the dogs for the night. One woman had moved though the hut scrubbing with the leaves. An altar of branches had been erected between the main posts of the house. The ritual boat which had been carved for the ceremony was placed in the center of the room. It had also been painted with *jagua,* with some of the same patterns that were now on my skin. A *kugurú* (large pot) of *chicha* had been made especially for the ritual. The figures of the ancestors that had been carved were also brought to the center of the circle that was forming. The child, whose face was pale and masklike from the bout of cholera, lay on a bed of leaves.

We entered and joined the others in the circle to wait for the shaman to return. When Loremiro entered, he set his *ambugé,* the ritual bench, next to the child, on the boundary of the everyday and the otherworld, as it had been explained. The shaman went to the boy and passed a hand over his form. The ceremony would begin.

In the distance someone blew the shell of a conch, and Loremiro began to sing. His song sounded like voices from the jungle, like birds or frogs, like water falling. He called on the *hai,* the animal spirits to come. "*Sönwända-numua,*" he sang, the words for "wings rubbing," which also means "curing" in Emberá. He shook the leaf fan made from *pärärä* leaves and tapped the floor with his medicine stick.

He sang of the boy as having lost his spirit in the river—*tadzi häüre doedá-besia* (our spirit in the river stayed). The boy had become sick from drinking the river. The river had hence taken a part of him away in the exchange. They were seeking to reclaim the child's lost spirit from the depths of the water. The people in the circle waved their fans as well, and the shaman continued, asking the boat, the *hampá,* to bring the ancestors. He sang of the boat navigating into the dawn, carrying the *hai* across the boundary. He asked for the aid of the ancestors to drive the sickness from the child, to navigate the boat across to this world.

When he was silent, it had grown too dark even to see his form, and he lit a small fire of leaves next to the child. He turned and spoke to the circle. "The pot of chicha has gone down," he announced. "The ancestors have come and drunk from the pot." The chicha was then passed around the hut, and everyone drank to the health of the child, who did in fact seem to be flourishing in the light of the fire.

247

54

ANA MARIA WAS a little worried about sending me home alone the next day, but she had to stay a few more weeks in Quibdo. She told me if I had any trouble with the boat at the dock in Jurado I should go see Don José, an acquaintance of hers and, ironically, the main wood-seller in town, or Neftali, who lived across the river. I could stay with either of them if necessary. But she didn't think it would be—I would probably catch the boat to Jaqué.

We parted company on the river; she went one way and I the other. We said a small good-bye. She said she didn't like good-byes and that it was best like this—quick, as the boats were leaving. We waved as the canoes slowly moved away from each other.

Both canoes were overflowing with people, mothers with babies, people going to Jurado for New Year's Eve. The canoe moved slowly, despite its motor. The boat was heavy in the water and kept scraping the bottom. In places the river was only ankle deep. We all got out, and the men dragged the canoe through the mud.

Everyone was quiet. An hour passed, and no one said a word, except to grunt and give some expletive about the canoe or the river when we had to stop. I was not used to such silence, but I didn't want to break it. The people were friendly to me, holding out bread to break off, or a piece of fruit. But we didn't talk.

I thought about Michael Ondaatje's character, Count Ajami, who told the tale of traveling for several days through the desert with an Arab companion who didn't speak the whole way, except for one word: he pointed his finger and said "Ghat" when they arrived. I once read a story about a man who had gone on a hunting trip with a friend who never spoke a word for four months. "That was a good trip," he said.

In the pace of my life back home, people rarely make room for silence. We fill up all the space with words, with appliances. Everything moves so fast. There is not enough time for the natural pauses our minds need for contemplation. Living in the city distorts our natural rhythms, breaks up time into quick little pieces, and we are divided along with them. Here, whole days would roll by with the sun, whole nights with the moon, and we hardly noticed the time passing.

But sometimes, there is a boat to catch. I was beginning to get a little anxious about the time, the delays caused by having to stop and walk so much, when the motor suddenly sputtered and died.

Somehow I knew it was dead for good when I heard the sound. I stepped out of the boat in the knee-deep river and looked at the sky. It was already about three in the afternoon. The boat to Jaqué would be leaving in about an hour, and we were still several hours from Jurado if we had to walk or paddle.

The men worked on the engine for a while. I sat on a rock at the edge of the bank, feeling the time slip by. There was no way I would make the next boat. I would miss all of my connections home. I had made the tight connections before I knew what it was like here—before I knew how uncertain any leg of the journey might be—before I realized how reliant we would be on the weather, or the tides, or a single boat and its engine. Finally, the men decreed the motor's death, and we began to wade through the river towards Jurado. We took turns, occasionally sitting and paddling, or walking the shallow places.

There was nothing I could do. I would have to stay the night in Jurado and hope for another boat out in the next day or two.

We moved quickly because it was important to reach town before dark. One of the women told me that if the guards heard sounds after the sun went down, they might begin shooting in the water. As it was New Year's Eve, they might be drunk on the dock and especially trigger-happy. "One time we came late with the canoe," she said, "and a bullet almost took my brother's ear off."

We waded on, and without the noise of the motor, the sounds of the forest and the river filled my consciousness. I gave in to the idea of staying in Jurado for the night. I would look for Don José or Neftali. I felt the world open up once I gave way. I felt the breeze cool my face, the water rush against my legs, the rocks under my sandals, the sun against my tattooed skin and, strangely, I felt prepared.

SEVEN

Neftali's Boat

Write the things which thou hast seen, and the things which are, and the things which shall be hereafter; The mystery of the seven stars which thou sawest in my right hand, and the seven golden candlesticks. The seven stars are the angels of the seven churches: and the seven candlesticks which thou sawest are the seven churches.

Revelation 1:19–20

55

WE ARRIVED IN Jurado just as the sun was setting. I was relieved. On the river, I hadn't known the distance farther and I didn't want to ask. The guards didn't bother with anyone on my boat. They did take a second glance at me, though—as an unlikely visitor.

The dock was empty. A few emaciated dogs eyed us as we unloaded, but they didn't come too close. We were too late for me to catch the connecting boat from Colombia to Panama. Ana Maria had given me the names of a few people I could stay with, in the event I arrived too late. I asked one woman about Don José or Neftali, and she said, "Don José . . . and Neftali, the man who is building the boat—yes. Both of their houses are all the way on the other side of town."

I thanked her and started off down the muddy road that, fortunately, had hardened in the day's sun. I could hear loud music playing from the center of town, mixing with the sound of generators. Jurado was a very skinny village, squeezed in-between the river and the ocean at the edge of the rain forest. Most of the village was built along one long dirt road, which had a short paved section. I wondered at the purpose of the paved patch, since there were no cars. Jurado could be reached only by sea or by a journey through dense rain forest. There were no roads out.

I passed a few stuffed figures that looked like scarecrows, which seemed strange in the center of town. The huts were built as close to the river as possible, and I could see that several people had planks extending out to little wood outhouses over the river. Just a few yards away, a woman washed dishes in the river, and another bathed her baby.

Near the end of the road, a church stood tall in comparison to all the one-room huts. I stopped short when I saw it—the cross on the steeple was upside down. No mistaking it. I felt a chill run through my body as I wondered what it could possibly mean.

A woman was passing me on my right. "The cross," I said, pointing. "It's upside down."

She looked up. "Yes," she said, as if she were surprised that I would think this strange or unusual. "It's been that way for a while. There was another one, a beautiful one, but some years ago, before I was here, they say a great wind blew through and blew the cross into the ocean. Then they put this one up there, and at some point over the years, it flipped over. The roof is old and very dangerous, so no one wants to climb up there and fix it. Anyway, most people don't really notice it's upside down anymore."

I had looked up Jurado in my dictionary and knew the name meant "sworn enemy," but it was also a word for jury. Ironic, I had thought, trying to make sense of the double meaning of the word. Later, Ricardo had told me that the name Jurado actually came from the Cuna: the name for Cuna in their own language was *Jura* and *Do* meant land or water. So the town's name meant "land or water of the Cuna people." The Cuna, however, had mostly been pushed North into regions now belonging to Panama.

Jurado is not marked on many newer maps of Colombia. Older maps of the region, from the 1700s, for instance, show the River Urado where the town exists. It is an often-forgotten place, transitory—its size changes with the seasons that flood and drain the land. It changes with the tides.

Like many of the settlements on the Pacific coast of Colombia, the village had been formed by runaway slaves, most fleeing the gold mines of Chocó. Escaped slaves or *cimarrones,* as they were called, had lived there for hundreds of years in a tense coexistence with the native Emberá, whose culture struggled to remain intact. In the last thirty years, drug money had moved through the town, and a bank was created. Guerrillas robbed the bank in the 1980s as an action explicitly directed against drug money, they said, and the government set up an army base on the edge of the village on the most beautiful stretch of beach, virtually penning the people in the town.

The people of Jurado have gradually lost all sources of income—they live in town and only a very few have land to grow their own food on. The newest exploitation of the last ten years has been of the trees, the wealth of the Chocó region, this strip of forest between the Andes and the Pacific.

I reached Don José's house, which I knew immediately because he was the richest man in town—he owned the lumberyard. Most of the people of Jurado lived in huts with no running water, but Don José's house was a sturdy construction of oak and mahogany with several rooms and a porch.

Don José also owned the ice-making plant, which was located in a building next to his house. A long line of people who had come for ice stretched into the street.

A small child, having just collected her family's ice, stood waiting for her mother to return. She was holding the block of ice on her head, and it had begun to melt, trickling down the side of her face. She looked anxiously in the direction her mother had gone and shuffled her bare feet in the dirt. When her mother suddenly reappeared, her face broke into a smile. She said, *"Lo tengo,"* telling her mother she already had it. The mother nodded, a basket of bananas on her head. She and the child walked down the road towards home, the child shivering a little beneath the burden.

The ice glistened as she passed me, and its sides reflected the world around: her mother on the left with the load of bananas, to the right, men in the lumberyard with their chain saws, the sky above turning colors in the sunset, and in the side turned towards me, I could see my own reflection.

At the lumberyard, the party for the New Year had already begun. The music was playing louder and louder, and people were beginning to dance in the streets or, rather, on the dirt path. The waiting customers pushed forward to be assured of their ice. I went to the gate of Don José's house, where a man met me almost immediately.

The music blared in the background, and I had to ask him to repeat himself a few times. "Don José?" he asked. "He's in Bahia Solano for the New Year. He won't be back for several days. But you must join us anyway."

I looked inside at the wild party, consisting mostly of drunk men, and declined the invitation. I thanked him but asked instead about where I could find Neftali. "Neftali?" He gave me a funny look. *"El loco?"* He pointed across the river.

In the low light, I could barely make out a house on stilts with what looked like a boat under it. "I don't know if he's there," the man said. "You can call across the river—when those chain saws stop going." I nodded nervously, peering down to the river where his finger pointed. The dusk gave everything an unearthly hue as I walked slowly down to the edge of the water.

A huge barge headed for Buenaventura, a town down the coast, was up on land because the tide was out. The barge was so wide that it hardly seemed as though it would fit in the river. I watched as a man carrying a section of tree at least four times his height staggered under its weight. Waist-deep in the water, he lowered his body to get a better grip. He hoisted the log onto his shoulder and dragged it out of the water, through the mud, and up the plank of the ship.

Another group of men were simultaneously operating chain saws to shorten some of the already dry logs. The scream of all the saws at once filled the air and drowned out the music at the house and the people's voices. I looked back to the river, where several other men were emerging, walking very slowly under the great weight. One after another, they came out of the river and headed up into the barge, carrying the logs like crosses on their shoulders. They returned to the river for another and another, moving like an assembly line.

I'm not sure how long I stood watching them, waiting for the sound of the chain saws to die down. This was the edge of town and had probably been the first part to be logged. There was only one tree left on this side of the bank, as far as one could see, and it shielded me somewhat from the men's vision. On the other side, where Neftali's house stood, the roots of the trees still held the earth together. But on this side, with no trees, the banks were eroding and the earth was falling into the river even as I stood there.

I had been unable to hear even my own voice under the scream of the chain saws, but the sound suddenly stopped— first one saw, then another, and then silence. At first, the silence seemed louder than the chain saws because it had come on so quickly. In the dimming light, the assembly of men stopped. They were calling it a day—a year, actually, as it was New Year's Eve. The last logs had been pulled from the river and were stacked in piles on the barge and beside it.

In the silence then, I stood at the edge of the bank a few more minutes, staring into the river and at the outline of the house and wondered how I should call for Neftali. Would my voice carry across the river?

Just then I felt a hand touch my shoulder. A thin, wiry, middle-aged man with a mustache and very dark, intense eyes asked, "You are looking for me?"

I was startled, but for some reason, his presence had a calming effect on my senses. "Yes," I said. "Thank God. Ana Maria sent me." At the mention of Ana Maria's name, his face became clear with understanding, and he nodded.

"I missed the boat to Jaqué," I told him. "I was returning from the Emberá village, and the canoe's motor broke down. But I have to be back in Jaqué to catch the plane."

"Don't worry about that," he said, "I know for sure there is a motorboat leaving for Panama tomorrow at dawn. But first, you must be hungry."

"Actually, I'm exhausted. I feel like I could lie down right here and go to sleep."

"Then you must sleep," he said, putting my bag into a small canoe to take me across the river to his house. "But I will wake you at midnight. It's not a good idea to sleep through the New Year. What you are doing when the year changes marks what the year will hold for you."

He poled the canoe across the river into the belly of the night. The canoe felt like a hollowed-out husk floating in the dark water toward the little house. I was too tired to ask about the ship underneath his house, whose bow arched from between the stilts. He brought me up the wood stairs, pointing out where some planks had been removed, "for a part of the boat," he said, and told me to be careful not to fall through.

A hammock was strung across the house, which had no walls, and I noticed that spiders had spun huge webs to catch any insects flying or swept into the house by the wind. The hammock swayed, and the stilts creaked slightly. I was so tired from wading all day through the river that I fell almost immediately into a deep slumber.

56

I woke in the hour before midnight, wondering where I was. Neftali was carving something. He held it out to me.

"Is it a bull?" I asked.

"Buffalo," he answered. "I've carved a bull, but this is a buffalo. You know about buffalo?"

A single book lay on a wooden chest, open to the page with the buffalo. It was the B volume of the encyclopedia. He said he had found it in a box of old magazines down at the village general store.

"Billy the Kid," he said. "You know about Billy the Kid? I was like Billy the Kid. But I didn't kill anyone. And I didn't die at twenty-one. But I left everything behind and went West. But this is as far as I could go. Without a boat, that is."

"And Lord Byron, the poet? You know him? Have you read his 'Fugitive Pieces'?"

I couldn't say that I had. He hadn't either, but he went on through Byron, Brontë, Beowulf, Brazil, Beelzebub, and John the Baptist, showing me pictures on several of the pages and some unfinished carvings.

He turned the pages of the encyclopedia to *barco* and showed me the different ships depicted. "I carved small ones first," he said, "but the one underneath the house I have been working on by daylight these last few years. She's taking her time."

"What kind of boat is it?" I asked.

"A Viking boat," he answered, and paused a moment as he blew some wood shavings off his hand. "There was a *Reader's Digest* that ended up in town some time ago, with complete blueprints for a Viking boat. I studied the design for hours."

He paused again, as if wondering whether to continue. "That night I dreamt about the boat," he went on. "I dreamt that *El Señor* spoke to me and said this would be my task here—to build this boat. But the next day the *Digest* had disappeared, so I was left to build the boat from memory. I guess *El Señor* wanted me to have an even greater task."

Back home, I probably would have thought, as the others in town seemed to, that the man was indeed *loco*. But I had seen and heard such strange things for many weeks now during this trip that his talk hardly surprised me. I thought of a statement Gabriel Garcia Marquez once made—that he makes nothing up in his stories, that he just writes down what happens and what the people tell him. I had begun to believe him.

"Of course, everyone here thinks I'm crazy—building this boat," Neftali continued. "But I'm sure they thought I was crazy when I first arrived. One day I just walked west from Medellín. I had to go through Chocó for many months, living off berries and leaves and what I could find. When I got here, I must have looked like an animal—half-naked, dirty, hairy-faced. I had to stop in Jurado because it's the edge. Actually, that's the way most of the people ended up in this town."

He was referring to the fact that most of the town's inhabitants were descended from escaped slaves who had fled through the forest until they reached the ocean and could go no further.

"Why did you build your house on this side of the river?" I asked.

"Did you see the other side?" he asked. "I like to have at least this much water between here and there. Actually, I'd like a lot more water, but this will have to do for now. I've been building the boat piece by piece. I'll trade sometimes for a certain piece of wood. But mostly, I've been using the house." He pointed to the missing planks.

"Where are you planning to go when you finish it?" I asked.

There was a long silence, with only the faint sound of the carving knife over the wood, before he answered that time. *"Cualquier viaje"* (whichever voyage), he said.

But before I could ask him more, we heard the voices from across the river rise to a new level, and he sprang up and ran to the edge of the house.

"It is the countdown," he said. *"El Año Viejo* (the old year) is about to be lit on fire."

I looked across the river to the party on shore, where one of the straw men stood tied to a pole, and all the people gathered around and began to chant: *"Diez, nueve, ocho, siete, seis, cinco, cuatro, tres, dos, uno!"*

At the turn of the year, the straw man was set on fire and burst suddenly into flames. All around town, fires began simultaneously as each party's effigy was burned. The people cheered and chanted and began to dance around the fires.

"Would you like to see her?" Neftali asked suddenly, pointing down to the boat.

Of course I did, and carrying two lanterns against the darkness, he led me down the planks and temporary stairs to the huge ship under the house. We went in through a small opening like an entrance to a cave, and the lanterns swung back and forth, casting our shadows on the skeleton of the ship.

"How long have you been building it?" I asked.

"Un tiempo," he answered, as if an exact time had no meaning.

We stood in silence in the boat as I wondered what other questions to ask him and whether I should ask at all.

Though on land, the boat creaked, and I almost thought I felt it move as if on water. Perhaps it was the wind whistling through the wood and blowing against the planks like waves. I could almost feel the boat straining to leave on some journey.

Walking inside the body of this boat built with such careful attention, I understood. It was a response to a calling—the shape of which we often cannot understand until we have reached the heart of it. Neftali had two books that directed his life, and while they were rather odd texts (the *Reader's Digest* and the B volume of the encyclopedia), he took their messages on faith. Even from my Western, "rational" perspective, I believe that certain books and experiences and people come our way when we need them. Fate hands us such tickets, and it is up to us whether or not we use them, even if we often don't know exactly where we are heading.

When Neftali told me his story that night, he left much out. But his actions felt prophetic. His faith felt prophetic. Perhaps, as various philosophers have described it, the major activity of the prophet is interference, to interfere with the way things are going: militarism, racism, materialism, environmental destruction. Jeremiah talks of the "tearing up and knocking down" which must precede the building up and planting. In much the same way a flood, though destructive, clears the way for new growth. As Neftali was taking his house apart, so had I been taking apart some of the structures and preconceptions of my life as a result of this journey. His house, like mine, was slowly being disassembled and put back together in a different form, one with a helm and a compass.

The hull of Neftali's unfinished boat curved around me that New Year, oval like an egg or a seed, holding me for that moment in time. Of course, I couldn't help but think of the Ark in the Bible, which I have long understood as such a seed, containing and preserving the messages of life until the new ground is prepared. The boat contained me as I became part of that seed, part of that story, which would help me begin to understand the pace and shape of my own.

57

A SMALL BOAT waited at the dock the next morning. It didn't have a name. Two of Momento's seven sons were making the boat ready. They all looked so much alike that it was hard to tell them apart. And I had confused their names, though I remembered they had all been named for angels and saints. That detail was hard to forget. I recognized Archangel, who had brought us across the border, but I didn't know his brother. They placed my bags in the bottom of the boat with the others and helped me on board.

"And which saint are you," I asked, half-joking.

The brothers laughed, used to the question.

"Santiago," he answered, and pushed the boat off from the riverbank.

As we moved down the river in the morning light, we passed the houses and the people waking on one side and the trees lining the bank on the other, going slowly until we reached the mouth of the ocean. The smell of the river and the town suddenly became fresh salt spray and air, and I turned my head to look behind. The village was growing smaller and smaller as we moved forward, the waves wild white horses gathering speed, until the huts and the people were once again indistinguishable from the land and the trees.

NOTES

CHAPTER 5

[1] Ivan Musicant, *The Banana Wars* (New York: Macmillan, 1990), 116.
[2] Ibid., 119.
[3] Quoted in Eduardo Galeano, *Open Veins of Latin America,* trans. Cedric Belfrage (New York: Monthly Review, 1973), 121.
[4] Ibid.
[5] Ibid.
[6] Eduardo Galeano, *Memory of Fire,* vol. 2, *Faces and Masks,* trans. Cedric Belfrage (New York: Pantheon, 1987), 237.
[7] Ibid.

CHAPTER 7
[1] World Commission on Environment and Development, *Our Common Future* (Oxford, UK, and New York: Oxford University Press, 1987), 114–15.
[2] David Suzuki and Peter Knudtson, *Wisdom of the Elders* (New York: Bantam, 1992), 22.

CHAPTER 24
[1] Quoted in Michael Taussig, *Shamanism, Colonialism, and the Wild Man* (Chicago: University of Chicago Press, 1987), 76.
[2] Quoted in Taussig, 69.
[3] Quoted in Taussig, 75.

Notes

CHAPTER 33

[1] Galeano, *Open Veins of Latin America*, 116–17.

CHAPTER 34

[1] Quoted in Richard Price, *Maroon Societies: Rebel Slave Communities in the Americas* (Baltimore: Johns Hopkins UP, 1979), 74–75.
[2] Price, 81.

CHAPTER 35

[1] Quoted in Galeano, *Open Veins of Latin America*, 23-24.
[2] Ibid., 24.
[3] Ibid.
[4] Ibid.
[5] *El Dorado: The Gold of Ancient Colombia* (New York: Center for Inter-American Relations), 17.

CHAPTER 36

[1] William Sharp, *Slavery on the Spanish Frontier: The Colombian Chocó 1680–1810* (Norman: U Oklahoma P, 1976), 13.
[2] Quoted in Sharp, 48.
[3] Sharp, 49.
[4] Ibid., 52.
[5] Galeano, *Memory of Fire/Faces and Masks*, 12.
[6] Quoted in Taussig, 298.

CHAPTER 39

[1] Quoted in Galeano, *Open Veins of Latin America*, 123.
[2] Ibid.
[3] Gabriel Garcia Marquez, *One Hundred Years of Solitude* (New York: Avon, 1970), 287.
[4] Galeano, *Open Veins of Latin America*, 122.
[5] Ibid., 114.
[6] Ibid., 115.
[7] Quoted in Galeano, *Open Veins of Latin America*, 116.
[8] Quoted in Naipaul, 87.
[9] V. S. Naipaul, *The Middle Passage* (London: Andre Deutsch, 1962), 182–83.
[10] Aldo Leopold, *A Sand County Almanac* (New York: Oxford University Press, 1966), 237–38.

CHAPTER 41

[1] Quoted in Galeano, *Open Veins of Latin America*, 155.

CHAPTER 47

[1] Alfred W. Crosby, *Ecological Imperialism: The Biological Expansion of Europe, 900–1900* (Cambridge, UK: Cambridge University Press, 1986), 17.
[2] Quoted in Crosby, 23.
[3] Galeano, *Memory of Fire,* vol. 2, 34.
[4] Quoted in Crosby, 185.
[5] Quoted in Herman Viola and Carolyn Margolis, *Seeds of Change: Five Hundred Years Since Columbus* (Washington, DC: Smith University Press, 1991), 108.
[6] Quoted in Crosby, 185.
[7] Crosby, 184.
[8] Ibid., 183.
[9] Ibid., 186.

CHAPTER 49

[1] Quoted in M. L. Duran-Reynals, *The Fever Bark Tree* (New York: Doubleday, 1946), 91.
[2] Quoted in W. E. van Heyningen and John Seal, *Cholera: The American Scientific Experience* (Boulder, CO: Westview Press, 1983), 12.
[3] Quoted in Laurie Garrett, *The Coming Plague: Newly Emerging Diseases in a World Out of Balance* (New York: Farrar, Straus and Giroux, 1994), 562.
[4] Quoted in Garrett, 50.

CHAPTER 52

[1] Taussig, 262.
[2] Eduardo Galeano, *Memory of Fire,* vol. 3, *Century of the Wind,* trans. Cedric Belfrage (New York: Pantheon, 1988), 14.
[3] Quoted in Taussig, 263.

SOURCES

Basho, Matsuo. *The Narrow Road to the Deep North and Other Travel Sketches*. Trans. Nobuyuki Yuasa. New York: Penguin, 1966.

Campbell, Joseph. *The Hero with a Thousand Faces*. New Jersey: Princeton University Press, 1973.
———. *The Power of Myth*. New York: Doubleday, 1988.

Carson, Rachel. *Silent Spring*. New York: Houghton Mifflin, 1962.

Center for Inter-American Relations. *El Dorado: The Gold of Ancient Colombia*. New York: Center for Inter-American Relations, 1974.

Chatwin, Bruce. *The Songlines*. New York: Penguin, 1987.

Crosby, Alfred W. *Ecological Imperialism: The Biological Expansion of Europe, 900–1900*. Cambridge, UK: Cambridge University Press, 1986.

Duran-Reynals, M. L. *Fever Bark Tree: The Pageant of Quinine*. New York: Doubleday, 1946.

Galeano, Eduardo. *Open Veins of Latin America: Five Centuries of the Pillage of a Continent*. Trans. Cedric Belfrage. New York: Monthly Review, 1973.
———. *Memory of Fire*, vol. 2, *Faces and Masks*. Trans. Cedric Belfrage. New York: Pantheon, 1987.
———. *Memory of Fire*, vol. 3, *Century of the Wind*. Trans. Cedric Belfrage. New York, Pantheon, 1988.

————. *Walking Words*. Trans. Mark Fried. New York: Norton, 1995.

Garrett, Laurie. *The Coming Plague: Newly Emerging Diseases in a World Out of Balance*. New York: Farrar, Straus and Giroux, 1994.

Leeming, David. *The World of Myth*. New York: Oxford University Press, 1990.

Leopold, Aldo. *A Sand County Almanac*. New York: Oxford University Press, 1966.

Marquez, Gabriel Garcia. *One Hundred Years of Solitude*. New York: Avon, 1970.

Musicant, Ivan. *The Banana Wars*. New York: Macmillan, 1990.

Naipaul, V. S. *The Middle Passage*. London: Andre Deutsch, 1962.

Pearce, Jenny. *Colombia: Inside the Labyrinth*. London: Latin America Bureau, 1990.

Price, Richard. *Maroon Societies: Rebel Slave Communities in the Americas*. Baltimore, MD: Johns Hopkins University Press, 1979.

Sharp, William. *Slavery on the Spanish Frontier: The Colombian Chocó 1680–1810*. Norman, OK: University of Oklahoma Press, 1976.

Stevens, Thomas. *Dictionary of Latin American Racial and Ethnic Terminology*. Gainesville, FL: University of Florida Press, 1989.

Suzuki, David, and Peter Knudtson. *Wisdom of the Elders: Sacred Native Stories of Nature*. New York: Bantam, 1992.

Taussig, Michael. *Shamanism, Colonialism, and the Wild Man*. Chicago: University of Chicago Press, 1987.

van Heyningen, W. E., and John Seal. *Cholera: The American Scientific Experience*. Boulder, CO: Westview Press, 1983.

Viola, Herman, and Carolyn Margolis. *Seeds of Change: Five Hundred Years Since Columbus*. Washington, DC: Smith University Press, 1991.

World Commission on Economics and Development. *Our Common Future*. Oxford, UK, and New York: Oxford University Press, 1987.

About the Author

D IANE T HIEL IS the author of *Echolocations* (2000), which received the Nicholas Roerich Prize from Story Line Press, and *Writing Your Rhythm: Using Nature, Culture, Form and Myth* (2001). A new book of poems, *Resistance Fantasies*, is forthcoming in 2004 from Story Line Press. Her work has appeared in *The Hudson Review, Poetry, Best American Poetry 1999,* and other journals and has been reprinted in Longman, Bedford, Harper Collins, Beacon, Henry Holt, and McGraw Hill anthologies, including *Twentieth-Century American Poetry.* She received her BA and MFA from Brown University and has received numerous awards including the Robert Frost Award and the Robinson Jeffers Award. Thiel has traveled and lived in several countries in Europe and South America. She was a Fulbright Scholar for 2001–2002 in Odessa, on the Black Sea, and is on the creative writing faculty at the University of New Mexico. Her Web site is at www.dianethiel.net.

Transporting horses to the New World
(from an eighteenth-century manual)